REVIVAL RAIN

W. SAMUEL SANDEMAN

The faith building
40-day devotional

"Ask the Lord for rain in the time of the latter rain..."
ZECHARIAH 10:1

Revival Rain

"Ask the Lord for rain in the time of the latter rain…" Zechariah 10:1

Published by Every Nation Durban

Durban, South Africa

info@endurban.org

ISBN 978-0-6397-0695-5

ISBN (ebook)978-0-6397-0696-2

4 6 8 10 9 7 5 3

Illustrations by Rachel Nyman
Cover design by Thabo Moloi
Layout by Boutique Books
Printed in South Africa by Digital Action

Corporate businessmen in expensive suits kneel and weep uncontrollably as they repent of secret sins. Drug addicts and prostitutes fall to the floor on their faces beside them, to lie prostrate before God as they confess Jesus as Lord for the first time in their lives. Reserved elderly women and weary young mothers dance unashamedly before the Lord with joy. They have been forgiven. Young children see incredible visions of Jesus, their faces a picture of divine delight framed by slender arms raised heavenward.

**SENIOR PASTOR JOHN KILPATRICK,
BROWNSVILLE ASSEMBLIES OF GOD**

Dedication

This book is dedicated to my friend Karabo Mokoape, may your life be a seed that sparks revival. To Thuli, Somila and Samora; I believe that the sufferings of this present time are not worthy to be compared with the glory which shall be revealed (Romans 8:18) so may He give you strength and grace for the days ahead.

Thanks & Acknowledgement

To my wife and sons: Trish, Caleb and Daniel, who generously release me to spend time "in the Word" and who make my life the colourful and meaningful adventure it is.

To my BIG family of brothers, sisters, nieces, nephews, in-laws and parents who continually encourage me and believe in me.

To my local church of 20 years, I am what I am because you gave me place, space and grace to grow. Together we will see revival!

To Winston & Bronwyn Owen who read, edited and made this book a hundred times better than I ever could.

To Rona Miller who cast her expert eye on all the editing.

To the amazingly gifted Rachel Nyman, who did the beautiful illustrations.

To Thabo Moloi (my favourite DJ) who created the cover design.

How to use this Book

This book is a devotional journey that can be done individually but is best done corporately. We recommend that you find some friends and make a commitment to doing it for 40 days. Better yet, if you can get your whole church to do it every day for 40 days, we believe it will impact your community tremendously.

Why not add a fast?

You will also notice that we recommend you take the last three days of the devotional as days of fasting for revival—this is a powerful way to complete the book. Perhaps take a day to fast as you plan to start as well. We have placed some fasting tips in Annexure 1.

Why not add some sound?

If you visit www.40daysofprayingforrevival.com and submit your email address, we will send you an audio of each day's devotional… free of charge!

Why not add some ink?

There is space on each day for you to write your own thoughts and prayers; make this a book full of your own ink.

Need more copies?

You can order more copies by visiting our website: www.40daysofprayingforrevival.com. We have generous discounts on bulk orders to empower churches who would like to put a copy of this book in everyone's hands and take their entire community through this devotional journey.

INTRODUCTION

Not by might nor by power, but by my Spirit,' says the Lord Almighty.
ZECHARIAH 4:6 NIV

Welcome to 40 days of praying for revival

Let me start this book by making an embarrassing confession. I am the pastor of a local church and have been reading and teaching the Bible for 20 years. For most of that time I thought 'revival' was *'Christianese'*, you know what I mean, language that Christians use. Many churches call themselves something with the word revival e.g. 'Revival Centre' or 'Revival Life' etc. Also, where I come from 'revival' is often used as another word for a 'crusade' or an 'outreach'. I have often heard people saying after such events where many gave their lives to Christ that 'it was revival'. So, to be honest, I thought it was just another over-used Christian word like 'Hallelujah,' one that means God did something awesome or the meeting was extra special. Then, I did a study on revival and learnt that revival is actually a 'thing', a real 'thing!' Far from just another word, I would go as far as calling it an historical phenomenon. Let me explain…

Church history can be viewed as a series of movements or personalities who pioneered and advanced God's kingdom. We typically think of the early apostles blazing a trail through the Roman Empire or the church Fathers and their carefully articulated creeds. Luther, Calvin, and the missionary movements that followed with legends like William Carey and Hudson Taylor. There are too many to mention! These giants of wisdom, sacrifice, and courage carried the cause of Christ to nations and peoples. It could be said that we have what we have and know what we know because of them.

However, behind all these great leaders is the person of the Holy Spirit, playing the unseen and sometimes unknown leading role. Yes, the leading role. Think about Luther's transformative faith encounter or John Wesley's heart that was 'strangely warmed'— was that not the work of the Holy Spirit? Was that not the start of everything good? Could we ever quantify the work of the Holy Spirit reviving, leading, inspiring, guiding…? I think we would run out of verbs! Does anything significant happen without Him? Is there anything good in our hearts or the church at large that we cannot attribute to Him? Even His gentle whisper can change the course of lives and nations. Where would we be without that whisper? Imagine there was no Pentecost, where would the church be?

I believe that we cannot do any work of God without the Spirit of God and just as we accept the work of Scripture as 'God-breathed' though penned by man (2Tim 3:16) we must also see the work of God's kingdom in history as the breath of God through people. It is for this reason that I think church history is more accurately viewed as a series of revivals, large or small, corporate or personal. Yes, YOU can have a personal revival. Who knows what will come of that and how much the kingdom will advance? I bet that it will be significant!

The western church today is highly equipped. We have unrestricted access to the Word and biblical teaching on multiple platforms and in almost every language. We have discipleship tools for every situation and generation. We have seminaries, schools, and global conferences. We have growth strategy consultants and professional musicians. Have we ever been more organised? And yet as much as we can control the natural order or influence the human mind, will, and emotions, we are not able to give anyone eternal life or manufacture anything remotely close to the presence of the Holy Spirit and what the Spirit can do to heal and empower people. Pentecost proves this.

This understanding needs to sink deep. We cannot do the work of God without the Spirit of God. This truth needs to sink so deeply into us that it fundamentally changes the way we do life and ministry. It needs to change how we 'do' church and how we see progress. Our programmes have no eternal impact apart from the power He supplies. The only thing good about us is that God put His Spirit in us. And just as Jacob walked with a limp for the rest of his life post his encounter with God, we too need to walk with a crippled esteem of our ability and a leaning on and into the Spirit for the simplest of steps we take forward.

It is this revelation and subsequent disposition in the believer's heart that this devotional seeks to cultivate.

Forty days is a significant time in the Bible. The earth was purged by water for 40 days and 40 nights, Moses was on Mount Sinai 40 days, Jesus fasted for 40 days before the commencement of His public ministry, and He spent 40 days talking with His disciples before His ascension. Forty days is clearly time enough to be purged of the world, encounter God, and be transformed. I hope that the next 40 days will do this for you and for your church and that you will come into a high estimation and appreciation of the Spirit-filled and Spirit-led life.

This devotional is also in response to a growing global prophetic unction that revival is coming.

Revival is definitely "in the air." And not just any revival, a global (not local) revival, a mighty move of the Holy Spirit that will see a global (not local) harvest unlike anything else witnessed in history. In many places around the world, there is a prophetic alignment taking place with churches and movements that are sensing that something is coming and who are beginning to position themselves in prayer. Could it be that God is in this hour positioning His church for a global revival? I believe so and I believe this devotional will assist you and your community to align with what is to come.

Is there not a need?

In this devotional I define and elaborate on revival as having three core elements:

1. God coming near
2. The church coming alive
3. The lost coming to Christ

If these three elements are the historical blueprint of what revival is, then there could not be anything more important than for us to cry out for revival right now! Does the church need to come alive? Is there a harvest needing to be reaped? The state of the church and the state of the harvest are two big indicators of our need for revival and a quick survey of our current global reality should drive us to our knees in a desperate search for revival.

Why? Because despite our progress and ability in world missions there are currently over three billion unreached people in the world. The Joshua Project defines 'unreached' as people who don't have an opportunity to hear the Gospel because there is no significant evangelical Christian witness in their culture that can extend it to them. That is three billion people who will, in all probability, live and die without ever hearing the good news about Christ, the Son of God. These 'unreached' exclude all the nominal and lost people who are living all around us every day - they too are in desperate need of what we have… abundant life and eternal life. Right now, to use a phrase from Jonathon Edwards, they are "sinners in the hands of an angry God" or "children of wrath" as Ephesians 2:3 says.

Are these fields ripe for harvest or are they doomed for destruction?

Knowing Jesus's treatise on 'the lost' in Luke Chapter 15 and his unambiguous Great Commission in Matthew 28:18 we must believe that the fields are ripe for harvest, not doomed to destruction. It is coming time for global harvest. However, that does not mean we need to drop what we are doing and rush into the 10/40 window (The area between the 10 degrees north and the 40 degrees north latitude that contains almost 70% of the people groups that are considered 'unreached'). As I will share below, there can be no harvest without rain. We need the Holy Spirit. We need God to come near if we have any chance of seeing a significant harvest.

Does the church need to come alive? And by 'alive' I mean, does it need to be clothed with power and restored to its position of influence? Michael Brodeur in his book *Revival Culture* captures our current reality so poignantly with the following:

…the western Church has become ship-wrecked on the shores of this world system. It has found itself so bound by the tiny hindrances of consumerism, complacency, compromise, cynicism, and criticism that it has reached a point of paralysis and ineffectiveness.

Would you agree with that assessment? Many believe that Ezekiel's encounter with a valley of dry bones provides another vivid picture of the western Church today. It has structure and form in bones and bonds, but what it lacks is breath. It is a fully assembled army, but has no life in it. The church is a sleeping giant. The key to its destiny is the breath of God, not another book on organisational structure or how to live your best life yet. We need the breath of God. We need Jesus to breath on His people. We need the Holy Spirit, we need revival.

Signs of the Times

At the time of writing this devotional, the world lies in the grip of the COVID-19 pandemic. How interesting that suddenly we are one world. Whatever culture or nation you travel to (if you could travel there) we are all struggling through lockdowns and mandatory vaccines, wearing our masks wherever we go. The world has experienced a global wave of death and tragedy. For me, it's a sign of the times. A hint into the hidden spiritual mechanics at work in our destiny. Firstly, it is global.

Secondly, it's an attack on the respiratory system—an attack on our breath. With suffocating masks, oxygen tanks clanging in delivery trucks, and the short supply of ventilators, the word 'breath' is and has been *the word* for the last two years. Spiritually speaking it is in bold, underlined, and highlighted.

Thirdly, it's deadly. Global, breath, and death—what do we deduce from this?

It's the exact opposite of what we are prophetically sensing and asking for, which is a **global** outpouring of the **breath** of God that will bring **life** to millions. Global, breath, life! Coincidence? Could it be that in anticipation of what God has scheduled in an end-time global revival, resulting in a global harvest, Satan has caught wind and is running a-mock trying to drag the world in the exact opposite direction? A harvest of death before a harvest of life—sounds suspiciously like the circumstances surrounding the birth of Moses and Jesus. If you recall, immediately prior to the birth of Moses, Pharoah ordered that the Israelite babies be killed at birth. And after the birth of Jesus, when King Herod found out that the Magi had outwitted him, he ordered that all boys under the age of two in Bethlehem and its vicinity be killed (Matthew 2:16-18).

What a traumatic time of death and heartbreak that must have been for the Hebrews and Israelites! There was just no consolation for those mothers. As God was sending deliverers, Satan was at work to sabotage His plans.

This is how I interpret the last few years of death and heartbreak... an attempt to sabotage global revival. If we allow ourselves to be overcome by the despair of the pandemic and if we become spiritually weakened by the economic, social and political shaking we are experiencing then Satan's work is done. He will do anything to get us off course or to lose our spiritual position. And just so you know I am speaking to myself, this pandemic stole the life of my brilliantly gifted, young and very dear friend. I know the despair of this season. I feel the tug of hopelessness on my heart as you do too. But saints let us be awake and let us look beyond ourselves and see the plan of deliverance God is orchestrating in this hour.

God's End-time Revival Schedule

As mentioned above I believe the signs of revival are all around us. Has God scheduled an end-times global revival? I believe He has, and I believe there are a few clues in Scripture that can ignite our expectation.

Below are two Scriptures from two separate books of the Old Testament. Can you spot the pattern?

Then the Lord said to Moses, "Go to the people and consecrate them today and tomorrow, and let them wash their clothes. And let them be ready for the third day. For on the third day the Lord will come down upon Mount Sinai in the sight of all the people.
EXODUS 19:10-11 NKJV

God gives the Israelites two days to consecrate themselves and then on the third day He promises to visit them. Something similar happens in this passage:

Come and let us return to the Lord; For He has torn, but He will heal us; He has stricken, but He will bind us up. After two days He will revive us; On the third day He will raise us up, that we may live in His sight. Let us know, let us pursue the knowledge of the Lord. His going forth is established as the morning; He will come to us like the rain, Like the latter and former rain to the earth.
HOSEA 6:1-3 NKJV

Did you spot the pattern? Hosea is calling Israel to repentance and in doing so he is repeating the pattern in Exodus: after two days of consecration God will revive and raise them up.

Thereafter, what Hosea says is very enlightening for us:

Let us pursue the knowledge of the Lord.

- In other words, let us study God and how God operates.

His going forth is established as the morning;

- The sun rises every day; it is predictable.
- There is darkness and then light arrives. That is the pattern of creation going back to Genesis Chapter 1.
- The Jewish day starts in the evening: "There was evening and morning, the first day." (Gen 1:5).
- Hosea is telling us that God's ways are also predictable. We can discern how He works, as we discern the pattern of morning following evening, light following dark.
- A relevant example of God's predictable pattern is that He gives people time to repent before He judges.

He will come to us like the rain, Like the latter and former rain to the earth.

- Hosea then drops a revelation bomb: He tells us in what way God is predictable, he tells us how God comes to us.
- God comes like the rain, latter and former rains.

What does this mean? Well, in Israel there are two rain seasons:
1. The early/former or autumn rains: This is when farmers plough the fields and plant their seeds.
2. The latter or spring rains: This is when the crops are growing and the rain feeds them to maturity.

Now, there are also scattered rains in between during the winter months, but there is a significance about the early rains and the latter rains because they mark the start and end of the harvest season.

No Rain, no Harvest

Whether he knew it or not Hosea has given us a symbolic gem; a precious lens through which we can perceive God's pattern through church history. When we look at 2000 years of church history through the prophetic lenses he provided us with, we can see that it is an absolutely true picture of how God moves! If "rain" is symbolically the pouring out of the Holy Spirit and the "harvest" is symbolically the lost coming to Christ, then we see this predictable pattern. Without the rain, there is no harvest. This is constant enough to be mathematical in certainty.

This is why Jesus told His disciples to wait in Jerusalem until they were filled with the Holy Spirit. As soon as the Holy Spirit came, three thousand souls were added to the Kingdom of God. Interestingly, the Holy Spirit was poured out everywhere in the book of Acts, not just in Jerusalem. Philip went to Samaria and experienced an marvellous revival. Revival came to Cornelius's house. Revival came to Antioch and Ephesus. We see cities impacted and phenomenal miracles. Many believe that what we see in the Book of Acts is a former rain. A rain that announced the start of the harvest season.

From then until now we have seen scattered revivals all over the world. These revivals have broken up hard ground and created fields of harvest that are still blooming today. But they have all been local, not global. They have in many ways been like the scattered rains that pepper the winter months in Israel. This leads us to ask the question; could the winter months be over? Could there be a latter rain (revival) that will cause a huge harvest to come into the Kingdom of God?

Therefore, be patient, brethren, until the coming of the Lord. See
how the farmer waits for the precious fruit of the earth, waiting
patiently for it until it receives the early and latter rain. You also be
patient. Establish your hearts, for the coming of the Lord, is at hand.
JAMES 5:7-8 NKJV

In this passage, the apostle James is writing about the second coming of the Lord. I find it remarkable that in doing so he turns to Israel's harvesting cycle, mentioning again the former and latter rains. 'The farmer' is unmistakably God and the 'precious fruit of the earth' is indeed the harvest of lost souls. God sees the earth as a field of harvest, He thinks like a farmer, He is patient (it has been 2000 years), and like any other farmer, He waits for the early and latter rains.

Could it be that Jesus is not coming back until there is a latter rain and a harvest of souls?

This Gospel will be preached in all the world...
and then the end will come.
MATTHEW 24:14

And another angel came out of the temple, crying with a loud voice
to Him who sat on the cloud, "Thrust in Your sickle and reap, for the
time has come for You to reap, for the harvest of the earth is ripe.
REVELATION 14:15 NKJV

We have another pointer on this topic from the apostle Peter:

But, beloved, do not forget this one thing, that with the Lord
one day is as a thousand years, and a thousand years as one
day. The Lord is not slack concerning His promise, as some

count slackness, but is longsuffering toward us, not willing
that any should perish but that all should come to repentance.
But the day of the Lord will come as a thief in the night…
II Peter 3:8-10 NKJV

Again, Peter is encouraging patience, Jesus will come back. He is not slack, but He is long-suffering i.e. He is allowing time because He wants people to come to repentance. Furthermore, if a day is as a thousand years and a thousand years as a day then we could see the almost 2000 years of church history as just two days. Do you see any significance in that?

In Exodus and Hosea, we see a pattern of two days and then God comes. Hosea said, *"After two days **He will revive us**; On the third day He will raise us up, that we may live in His sight."* Revival after two days. Raised up on the third. Revival and then the second coming of Christ? I think so. We are due for revival and the earth is ripe unto harvest. We need the whole Church revived to reach the whole world.

Take a moment to meditate on these two Scripture verses:

…but truly, as I live, all the earth shall be
filled with the glory of the LORD —
Numbers 14:21 NKJV

For from the rising of the sun, even to its going down,
My name shall be great among the nations…
Malachi 1:11 NKJV

W. Samuel Sandeman

What should we do?

If you are still reading this, then God is pulling at your heart, and you may be asking that question: now what? What should we do? What can I do? God gives a simple answer:

> *Ask the Lord for rain in the time of the latter rain.*
> *The Lord will make flashing clouds; He will give them*
> *showers of rain, grass in the field for everyone.*
> ZECHARIAH 10:1 NKJV

In the last 20 years, we have seen a prayer movement birthed unlike anything in history. Global days of prayer, 24/7 prayer rooms, united city prayer, etc. It's another sign that the church is, at the leading of the Holy Spirit, positioning itself for end-time harvest. It is the time for the latter rain and by the Spirit of God we know it and so "the asking" has started. What are we to do in the time of the latter rain? Simple, ask for rain! Ask for the Holy Spirit to be poured out in this season.

Asking is necessary. In James 4:2 we are told that we have not because we ask not. In that verse, James is summarising the teaching of Jesus, found in Luke:

> *So, I say to you, ask, and it will be given to you; seek, and you will find;*
> *knock, and it will be opened to you. For everyone who asks receives, and*
> *he who seeks finds, and to him who knocks, it will be opened. If a son*
> *asks for bread from any father among you, will he give him a stone? Or*
> *if he asks for a fish, will he give him a serpent instead of a fish? Or if*
> *he asks for an egg, will he offer him a scorpion? If you then, being evil,*

*know how to give good gifts to your children, **how much more will
your heavenly Father give the Holy Spirit <u>to those who ask Him</u>!***"
LUKE 11:9-13NKJV

Many of us apply these words of Jesus to our daily needs. We are familiar with asking for better jobs, better cars, money, clothes, things, a husband, a wife, good health, protection on the roads, righteous leaders, the economy to turn, and so on. Don't get me wrong: these things are all ok to ask for, and God does give them, when asked. But here, Jesus is saying, "Ask for the best gift from your Father." Could there be a better gift than God the Holy Spirit?

This passage unmistakably emphasises perseverance in prayer with a focus on the Holy Spirit. There is a need for us to go through a process of asking, knocking, and seeking for the Holy Spirit. This is why I have written this book that you have in your hands. The next forty days will help you to focus on the miraculous, glorious, wondrous person of the Holy Spirit. It is designed to help you see our desperate need for Him and to cultivate in you a desire for revival to come to your own heart as well as your community. I'm praying that you have a personal revival in the next 40 days and that you become a 'spark' in your community.

Let's ask for revival rain because we are in the time of the latter rain!

Pastor Wayne

W. Samuel Sandeman

DAY ONE

Lord, send revival and start with me

Then, he lifted his hands toward heaven and prayed, "O God, are my hands clean? Is my heart pure?" Then, he went to his knees and fell into a trance. Now, don't ask me to explain the physical manifestations of this movement because I can't, but this I do know, that something happened in the barn at that moment in that young deacon. There was a power loosed that shook the heavens and an awareness of God gripped those gathered together.
DUNCAN CAMPBELL

Will You not revive us again, that Your people may rejoice in You?
PSALMS 85:6 NKJV

Take a moment to ponder where the world around you is at. Do you see in your society a genuine hunger for God and delight in His word? Is God famous and revered in your city? Is He the talk of your town and on the lips of those in authority? Is your Christian community powerful and influential, transforming the culture of commerce, schools, and government? Or does your world look the opposite of that?

Do you see people pouring into your church, asking how they might be saved? Are there any mighty signs and wonders authenticating the Gospel in your town? Is crime decreasing, are nightclubs emptying, and is there a steady flow of prostitutes coming to Christ?

The hardest question of all is: *'do we care?'*

It is possible that because we live in a world that has relegated God, His Word, and His Church to the outer limits of relevance, we can get used to being a minority without much influence. A small voice without much impact. We can even believe that this is how things always will be.

However, when we read the Bible we see God is meant to be number one; not just in the church, but in the whole world and every part of it. His Church is meant to be a city of light set on a hill giving light to all. Jesus came so we could be free in every way and God is not willing that any should perish. The last time I checked, Satan is a defeated foe and the gates of Hell should not be prevailing.

If ever we needed a vision of what our world should be like all we need to do is imagine what Jesus taught us to pray for:

> *In this manner, therefore, pray: Our Father in heaven,*
> *Hallowed be Your name. Your kingdom come. Your*
> *will be done on earth as it is in heaven.*
> MATTHEW 6:9-10 NKJV

'On earth, as it is in heaven.' This is the world as God intends.

But how? How do we get on the front foot again? How can we see our world transformed and looking like heaven? Glad you asked! Let me introduce you to… REVIVAL.

Revival is what God does when we start believing and praying for heaven on earth. He pours out His power through the Holy Spirit and changes the status quo. Revival is what happened in the upper room in Acts Chapter 2 on the day of Pentecost and then in multiple cities throughout the New Testament. In the last two thousand years, it has been happening in churches, towns, farms, university campuses, cities, whole regions, and even entire nations. Some revivals have been big involving multiple churches and carrying global impact. Some have been smaller with local impact— the world has seen revivals in many shapes and sizes.

Some have described revival as what happens when *"the veil between heaven and earth becomes thin."* I like that description because revival is heaven touching, transforming, invading, healing and refreshing earth.

When we understand what revival is and what happens when it comes, how it can literally transform our city and lives for the better and for generations, it can easily consume our prayers, it can easily become the most important thing in our lives and actually, it should be. heaven on earth should be what we seek first.

This is what this devotional is all about. Think of these pages as fuel to ignite your prayer life and set you on fire for revival. YOU can see revival in YOUR church and YOUR city!

Can you imagine all the chains that keep people in their sin and deception suddenly losing all their power? Can you imagine miracles breaking out everywhere, the lame walking, the blind seeing? Can you imagine mass deliverance? Thousands turning from their idols?

This is the book of Acts, this is the church as it was intended. In the Scottish Hebridean revival, people would repent in the streets and fields, no preacher or worship team present. In the Welsh revival, you could walk down streets and hear tears of repentance in people's homes.

Can we pray for this? Of course, we can! The question is actually: Why haven't we prayed for this? Why has this not been our number one all-consuming prayer? Did we not know it's available?

Did we not know it is possible? Or have we been too busy up until now? What have we been praying for? Is it really more important than revival? Could it be that WE need reviving?

As you commit to praying for revival for the next 40 days, know that you are included in this prayer because revival starts with YOU. Expect that as you pray God will indeed start with you and that you will experience a profound reviving of your faith and a growing passion to see heaven on earth.

And so we pray...

Lord, I bow my heart and bend my knee,
send revival, and start with me;
Pour out your Spirit in an unprecedented way;
May all who hear be saved today;
May all who are saved proclaim the Way;
Lord send revival and start with me.

Add some ink: *My thoughts and prayers on this day;*

_____

_____

_____

_____

_____

DAY TWO

God Coming Near

*When I speak of revival, I am not thinking of high-pressure evangelism.
I am not thinking of crusades or special efforts convened and organised
by man. That is not in my mind at all. Revival is something altogether
different from evangelism on its highest level. Revival is a moving of God
in the community and suddenly the community becomes God-conscious
before a word is said by any man representing any special effort.*
DUNCAN CAMPBELL

Is God just a powerful transcendent being that is far off, or is He also a loving father that longs to draw near to His children? We must know what we are asking for when we pray for revival. Our hearts can be emotional, we can be passionate, sincere, forthright, or maybe even desperate, but our minds must be clear and specific as to what we are asking for.

Some have defined revival as; *"An extraordinary outpouring of the Holy Spirit, reviving the church and drawing the lost"* or *"a divine assault on society, invigorating the church and converting sinners"*

Duncan Campbell of the Scottish Hebridean revival defines it as *'a move of God.'* I like that description! Revival is God coming down, God coming near. It is the outpouring of His awesome Holy presence and Spirit on earth.

Revival is a sovereign act of God that renews God's people through repentance and a fresh baptism in the Holy Spirit with major effects

on the whole community, or communities where it starts; the fire
of the Spirit then spreads out consuming all in its path! For God's
people, it's a fresh discovery of Jesus and a fresh baptism of Holy
Spirit fire, yet it is also God's response to the heart cry of his people
in prayer for their nation, their cities, their towns, their villages, their
local communities, their neighbours and their unsaved family!
REVD DON ATTENBOROUGH

When we pray for revival: we are specifically asking for God to fulfil the cry of Isaiah 64:1 which reads: *"Oh that you would rend the heavens! That YOU would come down!..."*

This is what we are asking for when we pray for revival! When God comes near as He did at Pentecost, we see two significant results:

- **The church coming alive**
  Which leads to all sorts of amazing things: missions, evangelism, devotion, worship, preaching, signs, wonders, etc.
- **The lost coming to Christ**
  This also leads to all sorts of wonderful things, including the decrease in crime, corruption, greed, prostitution, drunkenness, as well as marriages and families being restored, the community or larger society prospering, and the Kingdom of God being established etc.

These are the beautiful results or fruits of revival. These have been seen in numerous communities in various areas around the globe over all the centuries. They are the results of God coming down to be with His people, to establish His Kingdom and exalt His name according to His will and good pleasure. When we pray for revival,

W. Samuel Sandeman

we are asking for God to come near. Are you ready for that? Are you ready to encounter God in His holiness?

Before the Israelites were to go into the Promised Land Joshua exhorted them:

> *Consecrate yourselves, for tomorrow the Lord*
> *will do amazing things among you.*
> JOSHUA 3:5 NIV

Here is another Biblical pattern: Consecration comes before conquest. The purifying of our hearts leads to wonderful things, revival included. This devotion is a commitment to consecration. So, take time this day and every day of this devotion to confess your sin in whatever form it takes. Bring your heart back to the place where it sincerely and completely wants first and foremost God to come near, above and beyond any other want or perceived need we might have in our lives. This is the cry of revival.

And so we pray...

> *Lord, I bow my heart and bend my knee,*
> *send revival, and start with me;*
> *Pour out your Spirit in an unprecedented way;*
> *May all who hear be saved today;*
> *May all who are saved proclaim the Way;*
> *Lord send revival and start with me.*

Add some ink: *My thoughts and prayers on this day;*

_____

_____

_____

_____

_____

DAY THREE

The Blacksmith Prayer

*At the same time, the town of Arnol was awakened
from its slumber and captivity. At 2AM lights went on.
People came into the streets and started praying.*
DUNCAN CAMPBELL (REVIVAL IN THE HEBRIDES)

It's not uncommon in modern warfare, when ground troops are being over-run by enemy forces, to call out for air support to aid their efforts and put them on the front foot again. This is what we are asking for in revival, that God would come in the might of heaven's armies (aka "the Host of heaven") and 'rend the heavens.'

When we cry; *"Oh, that you would rend the heavens! That you would come down!"* we are asking Him to *'rend'* the unseen forces of darkness that reign over people's lives, blinding them from the light of the glory of the Gospel. The battle of advancing the Kingdom of God on earth is a spiritual battle and we need a spiritual victory before we can see change:

*For we do not wrestle against flesh and blood, but against
principalities, against powers, against the rulers of the darkness of
this age, against spiritual hosts of wickedness in the heavenly places.*
EPHESIANS 6:12 NKJV

*But even if our Gospel is veiled, it is veiled to those who
are perishing, whose minds the god of this age has blinded,*

who do not believe, lest the light of the Gospel of the glory of
Christ, who is the image of God, should shine on them.
II CORINTHIANS 4:3-4 NKJV

One such astounding example was the small town of Arnol in the
Outer Hebrides of Scotland. A stubborn little place with a small
population wanting nothing to do with the move of God happening
all around them. Blind people. Captive people. That was until a small
group of hungry believers began to pray in a farmhouse. A local
blacksmith was asked to pray and these are some of his passionate
words;

> *God, do You know that Your honour is at stake? You promised
> to pour water on the thirsty and floods on the dry ground. . . . I
> stand before You as an empty vessel and I am thirsty—thirsting
> for Thee and for a manifestation of Thy power... I'm thirsty to see
> the devil defeated in this parish... I'm thirsty to see this community
> gripped as You gripped Barvas. I'm longing for revival and, God,
> You are not doing it! I'm thirsty and You promised to pour water
> on me. God, Your honour is at stake, and I take it upon myself
> to challenge You now to fulfil Your covenant engagement.*

The story as told by many people goes on to say that:

> *At that moment, the house shook violently. A jug on the sideboard
> crashed to the ground and broke. Those who were present said
> that wave after wave of power swept over the room. At the
> same time, the town of Arnol was awakened from its slumber
> and captivity. At 2am in the morning lights went on. People
> came into the streets and started praying. Others knelt where
> they were and asked God to forgive them. Men carried chairs*

and women held stools, asking if there was room for them in the
church. Revival came to this last resistant town on the island.

Something happened when that blacksmith prayed. There was a breakthrough, a "rending of the heavens" and all those invisible forces that were holding people back from the Gospel were removed. Suddenly people could 'see', their hearts were suddenly open, they became God-conscious and repentance flowed freely. God had rent the heavens and God had come down.

When metal is cold it is hard, but when it is put in the fire it becomes soft and pliable. So, it is with our hearts. Sin makes us cold and hard but, when the fire of the Holy Spirit revival comes, those hard hearts are softened and bent towards God. How fitting that it was a blacksmith who was the catalyst for the breakthrough in Arnol. John the Baptist promised that Jesus would baptise with the Holy Spirit and with fire. Jesus fulfilled that promise on the day of Pentecost, and then again and again through the ages. He wants to do it again. Are you ready?

When we have done all that we can to share the Gospel and still we see no breakthrough in people's lives it is a sign that we need help, some 'air' support. There are unseen forces of darkness that are holding people captive to sin and Satan's will and we must turn to prayer and believe God to 'rend' those forces.

"Lord, make us like that blacksmith; so resolute, so determined, so bold, so precocious in his prayers to You! May we care for the salvation of our town as deeply as he did, may we press on in prayer like he did. May we care about the honour of your great name like He did. Let your name not be blasphemed amongst the heathen, but let your name be hallowed! Let your name be exalted on earth and in the heavenlies."

And so we pray...

Lord, I bow my heart and bend my knee,
send revival, and start with me;
Pour out your Spirit in an unprecedented way;
May all who hear be saved today;
May all who are saved proclaim the Way;
Lord send revival and start with me.

Add some ink: *My thoughts and prayers on this day;*

_____

_____

_____

_____

DAY FOUR

The Greatest Miracle

*Corporate businessmen in expensive suits kneel and weep
uncontrollably as they repent of secret sins. Drug addicts and
prostitutes fall to the floor on their faces beside them, to lie prostrate
before God as they confess Jesus as Lord for the first time in their lives.*
JOHN KILPATRICK (BROWNSVILLE REVIVAL)

Miracles are part of revivals and what great miracles happen when God comes near! In Azusa Street the walls were lined with crutches and canes, people came in bent, limping, shuffling, and left tall and upright, walking without aid. In many instances, nobody even prayed for them; they simply encountered the love of God amidst the congregation.

However, the greatest of miracles has and always will be the conversion of the soul. When the disciples came back with joy saying *"even the demons are subject to us in your name"* Jesus replied:

> *… do not rejoice in this, that the spirits are subject to you, but
> rather rejoice because your names are written in heaven.*
> **LUKE 10:20 NKJV**

The greatest show of God's power is not in how He triumphs over Satan. Satan has never been a match for God—ever. Rather His pre-eminent demonstration of power is that He can convert a sinner and bring that dead and condemned soul back to life, eternal life.

W. Samuel Sandeman

And you He made alive, who were dead in trespasses and sins...
EPHESIANS 2:1-2 NKJV

And you, being dead in your trespasses and the
uncircumcision of your flesh, He has made alive together
with Him, having forgiven you all trespasses
COLOSSIANS 2:13 NKJV

This is God's greatest and most important miracle! We only tend to appreciate it when we see hardened sinners converted, but even the most gentle and quiet conversion is still a miracle of magnitude greater than any healing we might ever see. Every physical healing is a celebration that lasts until the day of death. Though we see healings, those who are healed will still die one day because flesh and blood cannot inherit the kingdom. Even Lazarus, whom Jesus raised from death to life after four days in the tomb, eventually did die one day. However, to live beyond the grave is a miracle and demonstration of power beyond the world we know.

And all credit and glory go to God:

For it is by grace you have been saved, through faith
and this not from yourselves, it is the gift of God.
EPHESIANS 2:8 NIV

Salvation is the greatest gift—the greatest miracle. And heaven longs for more... more souls. Souls are the only treasure that can be rescued from the earth. They are the prize of heaven. Consider this:

- God does not want anyone to perish, but for all to have eternal life (2 Peter 3:9)

- All of heaven rejoices when just one sinner repents! (Luke 15)
- Jesus wanted and expected a harvest of souls; *'Look the fields are ripe for harvest,'* He said. (John 4)
- Jesus trained His disciples to win souls *'I will make you fishers of men,'* He said. (Matthew 4)
- In the parable of the lost sheep and lost coin—we learn no cost must be spared to find lost souls. (Luke 15)
- In the parable of the Prodigal Son, the biggest party is reserved for souls that were dead and are made alive. (Luke 15)
- In the parable of the banquet; we see any person will do: the forgotten, the broken, the poor, the destitute, the lame, the crippled—no matter what form they take, if it is a soul the person is gladly received by heaven. (Luke 14)
- The message of the incarnation of the Son of God is that heaven must be full of souls (Luke 15:24), no cost must be spared, even the blood of the Son of God! This is to the glory of God.

Revival, then, is God getting what God wants most: souls. If He is going to come near you can be sure it is not just for us to merely have a greater encounter with Him. He will make sure that when He comes, the saving of souls are on His agenda. If you do encounter Him in a wonderful way—as many do in revival—you can be sure that He won't leave you the same when it comes to your desire for the salvation of souls. So, if we are to pray for revival then we are to pray for a harvest: the salvation of souls. The two are synonymous and inseparable.

John Hyde the missionary to India prayed: *"Oh God, give me souls or I die!"* Such prayers cannot be ignored by God. When we cry for what is most important to Him it won't be long before He rends the heavens and comes to answer. And so, John Hyde prayed, sometimes days and sometimes whole nights for souls. Then in 1904 in Sialkot India, revival came. Thousands of lives were touched and transformed. People came to repentance. People accepted the lordship of Jesus Christ. People were saved. Precious souls were cleansed and forgiven through the precious blood of Jesus, the Lamb of God who takes away the sins of the world.

One witness said, *"The victory of the Sialkot meetings was not won in the pulpit but in the closet. Often the glory rested on these meetings in a mighty way, while hidden, out of sight, John Hyde and a faithful few travailed in prayer."*

Why do we so seldom ask for what is most sought by heaven? Why is God's agenda for souls so low on our priority?

Today we pray that God would give us His heart for the salvation of souls. Are they really important to us? Do we care where others might spend eternity? Behind every revival, someone carried heaven's agenda for souls in earnest and heartfelt prayer— let's be those people!

1 John 5:14 says: *"This is the confidence we have in approaching God: that if we ask anything according to his will He hears us."* Now that we know that this is His will, we approach God with confidence to pray.

And so we pray...

Lord, I bow my heart and bend my knee,
send revival, and start with me;
Pour out your Spirit in an unprecedented way;
May all who hear be saved today;
May all who are saved proclaim the Way;
Lord send revival and start with me.

Add some ink: *My thoughts and prayers on this day;*

_____

_____

_____

_____

_____

DAY FIVE

Audacious Prayer

*When God has something very great to accomplish
for His church, it is His will that there should precede
it the extraordinary prayers of His people.*
JONATHAN EDWARDS

There are different types of prayer. There is the quietly contemplative, intimate, meditative type of prayer that we can engage God with on a personal level. Then, there is also a wrestling type of prayer, a prevailing type of prayer, an authoritative, declarative, earnest, heartfelt, persistent type of prayer.

This is a type of prayer where the person has made up their mind. They know what they want and they will not be persuaded otherwise. They are not praying for things that are superfluous or things they don't really expect to see. Instead, they are asking as though this is the only thing they want.

These are Hannah's prayers for a child in 1 Samuel Chapter one. This was all she wanted. These are the prayers Elijah prayed when he was praying for rain, head down between his knees and sending his servant repeatedly to go and look for the answer to his prayers. These are the type of prayers that alter history. That bring breakthrough. That bring revival.

You could describe these prayers as **Audacious:** *brave, daring, fearless, unflinching.* I think we have done well to build contemplative communion with God, but if we are to pray for revival we must be daring and step into the arena of audacious prayer.

In his book *The Soul of Prayer*, P.T. Forsyth said the following:

> *Lose the habit of wrestling and the hope of prevailing with God,*
> *make it mere walking with God in friendly talk and precious*
> *as that is, yet you tend to lose the reality of prayer at last.*

Wrestling with God; prevailing with God? Do we know this type of prayer? It sounds like work, sweat, and aggression: do any of those words describe our prayer lives?

It reminds me of Jacob who wrestled with the Lord all night to the point where it seems God was willing to surrender: *'Let me go for day breaks'*, but Jacob dug in deeper *'I will not let you go until you bless me'*—how audacious! How assertive! Even aggressive! Modern Jews call it "Chutzpah".

What about Moses praying for the people not to be destroyed; God had to say, *"Now leave me alone so that my anger may burn against them and that I may destroy them...."* (Exodus 32:10 NIV) But Moses' prayers restrained and prevailed against God. Who did Moses think he was that he would step up and stop the arm of God? And yet he did! And even more bizarre it seems as though God was pleased by that!

> *Prayer hath the nature of violence; In the public prayers of the*
> *congregation we besiege God and we take God Prisoner, and bring God*
> *to our conditions, and God is glad to be straitened by us in the siege.*
> TERTULLIAN

This sounds crazy! Besiege God?? Bring Him to our conditions? Are you serious? And He wants that? For us urbanised, latte-sipping, democratic softies who type emails, such raw aggression and audacity is just plain foreign.

In the first century BC, a drought so bad threatened to wipe out a whole generation in the Holy Land. That was until a man of prayer called Honi stepped up to the plate. He took his staff and drew a circle in the dry ground and stepped into it. He got on his knees in the dirt and raised his hands to heaven and prayed:

Lord of the universe, I swear before your great name that I will not move from this circle until you have shown mercy upon your children.

How audacious is that! Needless to say, the rain came.

According to Scripture, there are no limits to how we can pray. In fact, it would seem that He expects and wants such prayer from us.

Which brings us to revival and clearly our biggest challenge with it: how do we get our hearts to break for it so that we begin to pray audacious prayers for it? Someone needs to flip our crazy switch and get us drawing some circles in the dirt and saying things like; *"Lord I'm not going to move until my city is saved!"* We need a holy hunger to grip our hearts, a raw, passionate craving for God to come near, for the church to come alive and for the lost to come to Christ.

And so we pray...

Lord, I bow my heart and bend my knee,
send revival, and start with me;
Pour out your Spirit in an unprecedented way;
May all who hear be saved today;
May all who are saved proclaim the Way;
Lord send revival and start with me.

Add some ink: *My thoughts and prayers on this day;*

_____

_____

_____

_____

_____

DAY SIX

The church as it was Intended

...For unclean spirits, crying with a loud voice, came out of many who were possessed; and many who were paralysed and lame were healed. And there was great joy in that city!
ACTS 8:7 NKJV

The church of God, being the Body of Christ, has and always will be at the epicentre of revival. When God comes near, souls are saved and the church is revived. The word 'revival' speaks of a *'bringing back to life'* or *'restoring to function.'* We see a pattern, throughout history, that there are seasons where the church loses its power, life, zeal, effect, influence, authority and it needs to be revived...restored to its intended function.

But revived to what? What should the church be in society? That nice building at the end of the street? Another option amidst other weekend activities?

Without a picture of what we should be and could be, we do not ever see our need for revival. Many modern church goers think that it is ok because they had a nice Sunday service: a good preach, good worship, a job well done. We think all is well because our worship team sounds great. We think we are ok because our church has a fantastic coffee machine, a friendly WhatsApp Group and our pastors are very hip. John Wimber used to say of church: "If God does not pitch up, we may as well stop and have coffee."

We get a picture of what God wants His church to be when we look at past revivals and at Scripture. When we see that picture, we should see our desperate need for revival.

Now it shall come to pass in the latter days That the mountain of the LORD's house Shall be established on the top of the mountains, and shall be exalted above the hills, and all nations shall flow to it. Many people shall come and say, "Come, and let us go up to the mountain of the LORD, To the house of the God of Jacob; He will teach us His ways, and we shall walk in His paths." For out of Zion shall go forth the law, and the word of the LORD from Jerusalem.
ISAIAH 2:2-3 NKJV

The church is meant to be the highest of the mountains—*exalted above the hills.* In other words, it should be the most influential and effective structure in society. Pulpits should carry more authority than any other platform; be it political, educational, or entertainment. Leaders of other mountains (government, business, media, education, justice, etc.) should be saying, *'let us go up to the mountain of the lord... so He can teach us his ways.'*

People should be flowing to it. Every church should have a river of people pouring into it and pouring out of it. Coming in lost, being transformed by the Gospel, and going out as disciples, missionaries, and nation-builders.

Church should be the place where we experience the presence of God; not just feeling His presence but seeing it through the Holy Spirit at work in people's lives. Where the Holy Spirit is manifest in a church or city, we hear these reports: *"evil spirits, crying with a loud voice, came out of many who were possessed; and many who were paralysed and lame were healed."* (Acts 8:7)

Church should be a place where you can be healed. Is anyone sick? *"Call the elders and let's pray the prayer of faith."* (James 5:14) Is anyone possessed or oppressed? Find a believer; *"for anyone who believes in Jesus will do the signs He did, they will lay hands on the sick and they will recover, they will cast out demons they will talk in new tongues."* (Mark 16)

We talk about nations being 'bread baskets'; but what of the words of Jesus to His disciples: *"You give them something to eat"* (Matthew 14:16) & *"feed the hungry, clothe the naked, if they are thirsty give them something to drink"* (Matthew 25).

Is this the church as we know it? Christians being salt and light, influencing the world with the love and truth and power of God? Or is it the world that is influencing the church?

When revival hit Azusa Street, a woman by the name of Jenny Moore fell from her stool as she was baptised in the Holy Spirit. She was a devout Christian before, but when revived she began to speak in new tongues and even sing in tongues—she sang like an angel. Then she stood up, walked to the piano and played it. Why is this remarkable? Because, she had never learned to play the piano in her life.

What a picture of what happens when revival hits the church. The church—that is believers—are empowered to live supernaturally and begin to flow in the gifts of the Spirit.

Philip was a deacon in the Jerusalem church, but when the Holy Spirit filled him, the Holy Spirit empowered him and moved him:

> *Then Philip went down to the city of Samaria and preached Christ to them. And the multitudes with one accord heeded the things spoken by Philip, hearing and seeing the miracles which he did. For unclean spirits, crying with a loud voice, came out*

of many who were possessed; and many who were paralysed
and lame were healed. And there was great joy in that city.
ACTS 8:5-8 NKJV

I would like to propose that we have not yet seen the church as it should be…

'A city set on a hill'; said Jesus. A city? Yes, a city—full of life, activity, power, ability, resource, ingenuity, flexibility, and impact. Jesus wants His Church to be a city within the city. We need to pray that God would send revival so that we can be the church that He has called us to be: the fully functional, empowered Body of Christ!

And so we pray...

Lord, I bow my heart and bend my knee,
send revival, and start with me;
Pour out your Spirit in an unprecedented way;
May all who hear be saved today;
May all who are saved proclaim the Way;
Lord send revival and start with me.

Add some ink: *My thoughts and prayers on this day;*

_____

_____

_____

_____

_____

DAY SEVEN

The Transforming Power of the Holy Spirit

*I felt a living power pervading my bosom. It took my
breath away and my legs trembled exceedingly.*
EVAN ROBERTS

Oh, the transforming power of the Holy Spirit! If revival is God coming near, then we are talking about God the Holy Spirit coming near. He is the third person of the Trinity. Jesus said, "It is better that I should go away because when I go, I will ask of my Father and He will send you the Holy Spirit." The Holy Spirit is phenomenal! He is the central figure of revival and when He comes, we are transformed!

This was prophesied by the prophet Joel:

*And it shall come to pass afterward That I will pour out My Spirit
on all flesh; Your sons and your daughters shall prophesy, your old men
shall dream dreams, your young men shall see visions. And also, on
My menservants and My maidservants, I will pour out My Spirit in
those days. And I will show wonders in the heavens and in the earth...*
JOEL 2:28-30 NKJV

The Holy Spirit is a wonder! When He comes, we are transformed: we prophesy, we sing, we see dreams and visions, we speak in new languages. He prays for us according to the will of the Father. We are filled with courage and boldness to proclaim the Gospel. And at the same time, we are also broken and cut to the heart for our sins and offenses against God. We bear the fruit of His character and are changed, becoming better people.

Evan Roberts a leader in the Welsh Revival of 1904-1905 had his own personal encounter with the Holy Spirit. He described it this way:

I felt a living power pervading my bosom. IT TOOK MY BREATH AWAY AND MY LEGS TREMBLED EXCEEDINGLY. THIS LIVING POWER BECAME STRONGER AND STRONGER AS EACH ONE PRAYED, until I felt it would tear me apart... I fell on my knees with my arms over the seat in front of me. My face was bathed in perspiration and tears flowed in streams, I cried out 'bend me, bend me.' It was God's commanding love which bent me and what peace flooded my bosom.

EVAN ROBERTS

Before this encounter he was a gloomy, serious personality. Afterward, he radiated tremendous joy!

Before this encounter he was a timid and hesitant speaker. Afterward, he spoke with authority and boldness. Before this encounter he was physically weak and couldn't walk far. Afterward, he could walk for miles to carry the good news, without growing weary.

What a transformation! This is the work of the Holy Spirit! It was after this encounter that he had a heavenly vision (*'your young men shall see visions'*) for a hundred thousand souls being saved. That is exactly what happened in the Welsh revival: over 100,000 people surrendered their souls to Jesus as Christ, Lord and Saviour of their lives.

Before the Ulster revival in Ireland, ministers described the church as: *'Dead to God, formal, cold, prayerless, worldly and stingy.'*

One minister said: *"I preached the Gospel faithfully, earnestly and plainly for 11 years, yet it was not known to me that a single individual had been converted."*

Then the Holy Spirit came to Ulster and they couldn't get people out of the churches. God's people became an army set ablaze with the Spirit of God—what a transformation!

In the 1857 revival in America, the presence and power of the Holy Spirit was so great over certain port cities that ships traveling to those ports would arrive with sailors contrite, broken and repenting and asking for preachers. It was as though the Holy Spirit had camped over the city and just approaching the vicinity was enough. Hardened sailors repenting? Sailors had a reputation in those days: like the characters in the popular "Pirates of the Caribbean" they were NOT the kind of men to ask for preachers; but the result of the transforming work of the Holy Spirit is sailors and sinners seeking God.

I think of Moses at his burning bush encounter with God and how he left a transformed man. If we want to see transformation in our lives, in our churches, and in our cities, then we need the Holy Spirit to come in all His might. The good news is that the Father wants to give us the Holy Spirit:

> *If you then, being evil, know how to give good gifts*
> *to your children, how much more will your heavenly*
> *Father give the Holy Spirit to those who ask Him!*
> LUKE 11:13 NKJV

The Holy Spirit is THE good gift. We must ask our kind and generous heavenly Father for that good gift with expectation. Do you need a personal transformation? Can you see the need for transformation in your church and city? If so, then let us pray for the Holy Spirit to come near and transform us.

And so we pray...

Lord, I bow my heart and bend my knee,
send revival, and start with me;
Pour out your Spirit in an unprecedented way;
May all who hear be saved today;
May all who are saved proclaim the Way;
Lord send revival and start with me.

Add some ink: *My thoughts and prayers on this day;*

_____
_____
_____
_____
_____

W. Samuel Sandeman

DAY EIGHT

Thirsty

...Out of his heart will flow rivers of living water.
JESUS

The Gospel of John records a dramatic proclamation made by Jesus at a pivotal moment in Jerusalem.

On the last day, that great day of the feast, Jesus stood and cried out, saying, "If anyone thirsts, let him come to Me and drink. He who believes in Me, as the Scripture has said, out of his heart will flow rivers of living water." But this He spoke concerning the Spirit, whom those believing in Him would receive; for the Holy Spirit was not yet given because Jesus was not yet glorified.
JOHN 7:37-39 NKJV

"If anyone thirsts let him come to Me!" Spiritual thirst is a prerequisite to spiritual renewal. No thirst no renewal.

When Jesus heard it, He said to them, "Those who are well have no need of a physician, but those who are sick..."
MARK 2:17 NKJV

A pre-requisite to healing is knowing you are sick. If you think you are healthy you do not need a physician.

And Jesus said to them, "I am the bread of life. He who comes to Me shall never hunger…
JOHN 6:35 NKJV

A pre-requisite to eating is being hungry.

Imagine that somehow there was a disconnect between your body and your mind and although your body was starving for food, thirsty, dehydrated, and sick—yet somehow your mind never knew it. You would never seek the water you so desperately need; you would never look for the bread that could give you life and you would never search for the physician that could heal you.

This is the condition of sinners before God: they don't know their true state. They have been blinded by the spirit of this age, so they think they are ok, when actually their souls are precariously balanced on the edge of eternal damnation. They cannot see their need for forgiveness, for a Saviour, for healing, for life.

Now, this can also sometimes be the state of believers. Somehow, we too can lose our first love, become cold, lifeless, and unresponsive to the Spirit of God. Maybe even proud and self-reliant, dare I say it; 'luke-warm.' The church in Laodicea (Revelation 3) thought that they were fine and wealthy, yet the Lord rebuked them and called them: '*naked, wretched, miserable, poor and blind!*' The answer to their condition was that they were to turn to Him.

To know our true state before God is the best place to be. Without it, we don't get what we need.

Could it be that we have become like the Laodicean church in Revelation 3; thinking we are fine, because we "prosper" but we are not? We are somehow disconnected from our true state?

Why don't we see Holy Spirit revival? The answer remains; *"Because we do not ask for it, because we have not seen our need for it."*

God fills the hungry and satisfies the thirsty (Psalm 107:9). *"Blessed are those who hunger and thirst for righteousness, for THEY shall be filled"* (Matthew 5:6). According to Scripture, the rain falls on the dry land. (Isaiah 44:3) If there is no realisation of our dryness we won't ask for rain. We also see that the fire of God falls on the sacrifice placed on the altar (1 Kings 18). With no sacrifice of prayer which requires time, we won't see the fire falling.

We don't see revival because we often don't see our ***need*** for revival. We must pray for God to show us our true state, to help us see ourselves as we really are. The truth is we and the world are in desperate need of revival. The land is very dry. People's souls are starving to death and desperately need the bread of life which Jesus offers. Without the living waters of the Holy Spirit, people's spirits are dangerously dehydrated.

Saints, let us pray that God would make us aware of our hunger and our thirst. Let us develop an appetite for revival. May we come to a place where we cannot live with anything less than thousands saved and the church restored to power and glory. When we have such a hunger and thirst, then we know the answer to our daily prayer for revival is near.

And so we pray...

Lord, I bow my heart and bend my knee,
send revival, and start with me;
Pour out your Spirit in an unprecedented way;
May all who hear be saved today;
May all who are saved proclaim the Way;
Lord send revival and start with me.

W. Samuel Sandeman

Add some ink: *My thoughts and prayers on this day;*

_____

_____

_____

_____

_____

DAY NINE

The Currency of heaven

*Everyone who **thirsts**, Come to the waters; And you who*
have no money, Come, buy and eat. Yes, come, buy wine
and milk without money and without price...
ISAIAH 55:1 NKJV

Thirst is a blessing! Hunger is a blessing! They are the currency of heaven:

Who can come to the waters? The person who thirsts. Who can come and buy and eat? The person who has no money.

In other words, who can have God in their life? Whoever sees their poverty without God can. Didn't Jesus say, *"Blessed are the poor in spirit..."*? Whoever has come to the place where nothing else can satisfy them and nothing else is as important as having God; these people can have God. Whoever has come to the place of realising that their entire strength, wisdom, and gift mix are not enough to watch the city and build the house—they are the ones whose cities God will watch over, and they are the ones whose homes God will build. Whoever has come to the place where the best, most comfortable, safe life the world can possibly offer is detestable and hated in comparison to the kingdom of God coming on earth. These are the people who inherit the kingdom!

Spiritual thirst, hunger, brokenness, and poverty are a blessing! They are the currency of heaven. If we have them we can make an exchange. Without them, we go without because we have nothing

W. Samuel Sandeman

to transact with. There can be no exchange between heaven and earth without them. We become window shoppers and spectators of the kingdom. Gazing in and watching God move, but never partaking and experiencing for ourselves.

Are we content to be spectators and window shoppers to the move of God?

This principle of being hungry and thirsty is a crazy upside-down principle to us because we live in a world that wants to eradicate hunger and thirst. Food and drink must always be within reach. We have vending machines, our petrol stations have convenience stores, cool drinks are sold to us on the beach. Hunger and thirst are horrible things to us. When we hunger we become irritable and tire easily; *'hangry'* they call it!

But in the kingdom it is the best thing, we become better when we stay hungry, we get stronger and more powerful, we become more spirit lead and we hear and relate to God better. It is as though we don't actually hear or receive from Him without it. It's when we lose our spiritual hunger or thirst and become comfortable, familiar, and satisfied that our spiritual demise begins.

The flesh and the spirit are complete opposites on the topic of hunger and thirst. In the flesh hunger is a problem, in the Spirit it is an asset! Spiritual hunger needs to be cultivated and looked after. It needs to be matured and become deeper and stronger.

So how do we do that?

- In the flesh, we hunger by ceasing to eat. In the spirit, we get hungry by eating spiritual food.
- In the flesh, we become poor when we stop labouring. In the spirit, we become poor when we start to labour and travail in prayer.

- In the flesh, we thirst when we go into dry places or we stop drinking. In the spirit, we thirst when we make a decision to leave dry places and barren lands and pursue God's wells, and start drinking. Drinking from the river of God makes us more thirsty for the river of God.

To grow in spiritual hunger we need to eat and drink as much as we can—the more fuel the greater the flame!

John G Lake said: *"When I approached this matter of the baptism of the Holy Spirit, I did so with great care, but I approached it as a hungry soul; my heart was hungry for God."*

For the next nine months, Lake sought the baptism of the Holy Ghost. He fasted, prayed, and shed tears. Needless to say, an incredible exchange took place and one of the greatest healing and apostolic church planting moves of God was born resulting in millions of souls saved and healed.

Evan Roberts said: *"I could sit up all night to read or talk about revival..."* And he did so for 10 years! Then a great exchange took place and he saw one hundred thousand souls saved in 6 months.

Hunger for revival is a precursor to experiencing revival. No one stumbles on revival by chance.

> *...I will give of the fountain of the water*
> *of life freely to him who thirsts.*
> REVELATION 21:6 NKJV

Saints this is the season to stimulate our hunger and thirst. Let us eat and drink as much as we can on the topic of revival. Let us labour in prayer until we are completely sifted and the only thing that remains is that we want God to come near, His church to come alive and souls to be saved.

W. Samuel Sandeman

And so we pray...

Lord, I bow my heart and bend my knee,
send revival, and start with me;
Pour out your Spirit in an unprecedented way;
May all who hear be saved today;
May all who are saved proclaim the Way;
Lord send revival and start with me.

Add some ink: *My thoughts and prayers on this day;*

_____

_____

_____

_____

DAY 10

Becoming the Prayer

Stand Mr. Campbell, for God has come. See what is happening.
HECTOR MacKINNEN

As much as revival is the answer to passionate hungry prayer, it is also the result of obedient and courageous people who are willing to step out, step up and take a risk to see God move. Maybe even become the prayer they have been praying.

As we pray for revival, we have to be keenly alert to anything the Lord might tell us to do, no matter how small, no matter how big, every obedient action counts. Every act of obedience could be the spark that triggers the *dunamis* (power) of God. Obedience is a key to revival. Being obedient to pray and also to act when called upon by Him.

Can you imagine Ananias of Damascus doing his 5am prayer vigil in the safety of his living room for the peace and revival of his city when suddenly the Lord appears to Him and tells him to go and lay hands on a notorious killer of Christians? He did what disciples do—he obeyed, and God did a mighty work in healing Saul of Tarsus and winning many to the Lord in that city. Ananias was willing to be the prayer he prayed. How willing are we to be the prayer we pray? Jesus gave his disciples a vision of the coming harvest, then he advised his disciples to pray that "the Lord of the Harvest" would send labourers out into the harvest field. Shortly

W. Samuel Sandeman

after that, Jesus answered their prayers by sending them out into the harvest field, giving them authority to do His works.

This brings us to Hector MacKinnen who was the postman on a small island of only 500 people. The island was called Bernera. It was in the Hebrides, off the coast of Scotland. Hector MacKinnen had become so disturbed by the spiritual ambivalence of his community that he took a day off work and committed the day to prayer in his barn. His wife recalled overhearing him pray for the preacher, Duncan Campbell to be sent to the island: *"Oh God, I do not know where he is, but you know and I ask you to send him."* At 10 p.m. that evening, Hector 'broke through'; he received a sudden and certain conviction that his prayers had been answered. So certain was he that Duncan Campbell was coming that he arranged accommodation and notified the whole community that Mr. Campbell would be preaching the following Thursday at 9pm! He had received the faith to be certain of what he hoped for.

At the same time, Duncan Campbell was at a large Christian conference in Ireland where he was the main speaker. Something began to stir in his spirit, and he sensed an almost irresistible compulsion to leave the convention and fly to the tiny Hebridean island of Bernera. It seemed crazy because the inhabitants of Bernera were less than the number attending the conference. But the compulsion was too strong to ignore. He did what disciples of Jesus do—he made his apologies to man and obeyed God.

Duncan left the conference and flew from Ireland to Glasgow and then from Glasgow to Stornaway (capital of the Hebrides). From there he drove many miles north, finally crossing the waters to Bernera on a small ferry. Stepping ashore at Bernera he approached a boy and asked where the nearest minister lived. The boy replied that both of the island's churches were without ministers at that time. *"Where then does the nearest church elder live?"* Duncan inquired.

"*In the house on the top of the hill*", indicated the lad. Duncan asked him to go and inform the elder that '*Mr. Campbell*' has come. The boy came back saying "*Mr. MacKinnen has been expecting you. He has arranged for you to stay with his brother, and you are preaching in the church tonight.*"

Eighty people came to hear the visiting preacher that night, but nothing unusual happened. So ordinary was the meeting that Duncan even wondered whether he had mistaken God's call and should really have been preaching to the large numbers in the conference back in Ireland. But God was not responding to the faith of the renowned revival leader, but to that of a humble village postman who had received certainty from God in prayer.

The congregation had left the building to make their way home, down the hill to the village below. Hector approached Duncan and sitting beside him said, "*Mr. Campbell, I hope you are not disappointed that revival has not come to the church tonight, but God is hovering over us and he will break through at any minute.*" Suddenly Hector stopped short, stood up, and slowly removed his hat. Gazing intently into the night he whispered; "*Stand Mr. Campbell, for God has come. See what is happening.*" There below them on the hillside, people were kneeling in the fields as loud cries of repentance began to fill the night air. The meeting, which had begun in the church, continued until 4am on the hillside. The whole community was gripped by a "*mighty visitation that shook the island from centre to circumference*" and every single household was impacted that very night.

Mr. MacKinnen and Duncan Campbell's willingness to obey and act was what made that revival possible. We too must be willing to obey as we pray for revival. No matter how big the action or small; a phone call, a gift, a seed, a message, an offer to pray… when Spirit led, these actions become doorways for God to move in extraordinary ways; especially when we are crying out for revival.

Will you make yourself available to God? Will you become the prayers we pray? See yourself as not just a "pray-er" of revival, but a vessel of revival. God has and always will use ordinary people to do the most extraordinary things.

And so we pray...

Lord, I bow my heart and bend my knee,
send revival, and start with me;
Pour out your Spirit in an unprecedented way;
May all who hear be saved today;
May all who are saved proclaim the Way;
Lord send revival and start with me.

Add some ink: *My thoughts and prayers on this day;*

_____

_____

_____

_____

DAY 11

Beautiful Repentance

Pale and trembling with emotion, in agony of mind and body, guilty souls, standing in the white light of that judgment, they saw themselves as God saw them.

WILLIAM BLAIR

There can be no doubt that repentance is one of the most pronounced manifestations of a revival. Can there be a revival without it? Definitely not! Repentance leads to revival (it's a key cause and catalyst to bringing revival). It is also an effect of revival. When it comes, revival leads to mass demonstrations of repentance in the most staggering ways. Usually, it is *the* sign that revival has come. Remember: revival results from the outpouring of the Spirit of God on societies or communities. The Holy Spirit, being the holy Spirit of the holy God convicts people of their sin, resulting in repentance.

What is repentance? Repentance is often understood as; 'a *change in mind*', or 'a *turning back to God*', or 'a *deep remorse and brokenness for sin.*' But none of these modern definitions do the word complete justice.

Most of the time we never fully grasp how grievous and hideous our sins are. I am *"a man of unclean lips living amongst a people of unclean lips"* (Isaiah 6:5). Sin in our world is legislated, congratulated, and even celebrated. But, when God comes near, suddenly we see ourselves as we ought to; our absolute depravity and desperate need for forgiveness and new life become real to us. We fall, we prostrate ourselves, we bow, we become as dead men, we bend our knees, we weep, we beat our chests, we confess. We empty ourselves of ourselves and as we do so, we are transformed and given new hearts; soft hearts; hearts of flesh. How beautiful!

Repentance is therefore a divine reaction that results in complete metamorphosis. How do I explain this in a way that gives it justice? It is the process and transformation from death to life and from sinner to saint. It is the process of new birth. It is the breaking of bondage and the loosing of chains. It is the conforming of our hearts to the heart of God. It is God pulling the plug on our dirty bathwater, all our detestable sin gets washed away and He showers us with His pure, brilliant holiness until every spot of dirt and thought that contaminates us is gone. It is miraculous and marvellous! It is the life of God being birthed in man. It is something that has to be experienced to be fully understood and God wants to do it in you:

> *I will give you a new heart, and a new spirit I will put within you. And I will remove the heart of stone from your flesh and give you a heart of flesh. And I will put my Spirit within you and cause you to walk in my statutes.*
> EZEKIEL 36:26–27

How important is repentance? We cannot receive salvation without repentance, and we cannot have revival without it! The Gospel is: *"repent and believe."*

- *"...Unless you repent you will all likewise perish."* Luke 13:3 NKJV

- Jesus commands *"all men everywhere to repent..."* Acts 17:30 NKJV
- Jesus preached: *"Repent for the kingdom of heaven is at hand"* (Matthew 3:2 NKJV). In other words we don't enter or experience the kingdom without this gift called repentance.

Repentance is a command, that is clear, but (get this!) it is also a gift. Scripture tells us that it is God's kindness that leads us to repentance. Repentance is similar to love. How? Well, love is a command in Scripture. We are commanded to love one another. On the other hand, God also gives us love for people as a gift and the result is we love as we ought to love. "God sheds abroad His love in our hearts through the Holy Spirit." How generous can our God be!

In the same way that repentance is a command, it can also be a gift from God. This means we can ask for it! And ask for it we should!

Repentance is typically not something we ask for. It is not high on our asking priority, but it should be because it is impossible to have revival without it.

God the Father poured out this gift of repentance in a beautiful way in Korea in 1907. A few missionaries committed to praying extraordinary prayers for revival and after just a few months their answer came. Around 1500 leaders and pastors from around the country gathered for a conference in the month of January 1907. A few nights into the conference there was an amazing breakthrough! The presence of God came into the meeting and one reverend came forward and repented for stealing. It was like the flood gates opened; man after man would rise, confess his sins, break down and weep, and then throw himself to the floor and beat the floor with his fists in perfect agony of conviction.

Sometimes after a confession, the whole audience would break out in audible prayer, and the effect of hundreds of men praying together in audible prayer was something indescribable. The next night the same thing happened, ministers even asked other ministers for forgiveness.

Presbyterian minister William Blair said the following:

It seemed as if the roof was lifted from the building and the Spirit of God came down from heaven in a mighty avalanche of power upon us... Every sin a human being can commit was publicly confessed that night. Pale and trembling with emotion, in agony of mind and body, guilty souls, standing in the white light of that judgment, saw themselves as God saw them. Their sins rose up in all their vileness, till shame and grief and self-loathing took complete possession; pride was driven out, the face of men forgotten. Looking up to heaven, to Jesus whom they had betrayed, they smote themselves and cried out with bitter wailing, 'Lord, Lord, cast us not away forever!'

The result of that encounter sparked four years of revival in the church in Korea. Seeing over 300 000 Koreans getting saved, churches being planted everywhere, prayer becoming the heartbeat of the nation, and missionaries going all over the world.

And so we pray...

Lord, I bow my heart and bend my knee,
send revival, and start with me;
Pour out your Spirit in an unprecedented way;
May all who hear be saved today;
May all who are saved proclaim the Way;
Lord send revival and start with me.

Add some ink: *My thoughts and prayers on this day;*

_____

_____

_____

_____

_____

DAY 12

Cut to the Heart

When I was seeking God for revival, I expected Him to start with the heathen, instead, He started with the biggest sinner of all—me.
ERLO STEGEN

Nevertheless, I tell you the truth. It is to your advantage that I go away; for if I do not go away, the Helper will not come to you; but if I depart, I will send Him to you. And when He has come, He will convict the world of sin, and of righteousness, and of judgment...
JOHN 16:7-8 NKJV

In what looks like a divine tag team; Jesus did His job, finished His race and as He ascended to heaven He 'tagged' with the Holy Spirit. The Holy Spirit left heaven and entered earth like a mighty rushing wind and tongues of fire. He filled the upper room and all the disciples, clothing them with power from heaven. Then, a crowd gathered—which is something the Holy Spirit does—He knows how to make an entrance and He knows how to draw a crowd. Then Peter preached under the inspiration and anointing of the Spirit. When the people heard the message, they were *'cut to the heart'* and asked what they should do; Peter commanded them to repent, believe, and be baptised.

'*Cut to the heart*'—this is what the Holy Spirit does!

He cuts past all our defences, logic, excuses, comforts, and apathy and He shows us who we really are before God.

Jesus said, *"He will convict the world of sin and of righteousness and of judgment."*

Sin, righteousness, judgment. He is after all the <u>HOLY</u> Spirit. He is identified and carries as His chief description the word HOLY.

It is obvious then that His main work is to bring people to repentance and typically that has to start with the church first (1 Peter 4:17). The church has always been God's chosen vessel through which the kingdom can come, but what if that vessel is unfit for a holy task? And a holy visitation from the Holy Spirit? The house of God needs to be cleaned and ready for a holy visitation before neighbourhoods, towns and cities can be reached. Conviction must come to us first. Repentance must start with us.

We are praying every day *'Lord, send revival but start with me'* and this is the right prayer to pray, because revival starts with repentance. And please note, He will start with you, calling <u>you</u> to repentance.

Just over 50 years ago a remarkable revival took place in what was then called, Zululand, in South Africa. A German missionary by the name of Erlo Stegen was working tirelessly in the town of Maphumulo. He had only 40 congregants. By all measures the ministry was completely ineffective, carrying no impact on the community or ability to see souls saved. So, they turned to God in prayer at 5am and 7pm every day. They studied the book of Acts together and they stopped all other activities. They were hungry and thirsty for a move of God.

Then Holy Spirit got to work: He began by showing Stegen the condition of his heart, which was filled with pride and racism. The times of prayer were focused on individual confession of sin, which at times became intense. Conviction led to confession as well as restitution and reconciliation. They were being swept clean and being made ready for a holy visitation. Then one day the Holy Spirit came like a rushing mighty wind and all they could do was bow and worship.

The Holy Spirit also began moving on the community all around them. People who weren't in the church were also overwhelmed with the conviction of sin. They couldn't sleep. They couldn't go to work. People were desperate to be freed from the burden of their sins. As if led by some mysterious hand, people began streaming to the Maphumulo congregation for prayer. Revival had come!

Thousands were saved from that move of God. There were also astonishing healings. They saw "sangomas" (colloquially referred to as 'witch doctors') coming to Christ and being delivered from demons. People burned their idols, charms, and amulets and turned to Jesus completely.

Erlo Stegen said the following:

When I was seeking God for revival, I expected Him to start with the heathen, instead, He started with the biggest sinner of all—me. Revival is not churches filled with people, but people filled with God. The Holy Spirit is not recognised through signs and wonders, but by His Holiness.

Saints, we must be ready for a deep work of repentance to start in our hearts. We must be expectant for the Holy Spirit to start with us, making us a holy vessel. Let no proud, racist, worldly, perverse, crooked, lazy, greedy, lustful, harmful, dishonouring, arrogant way remain in us! If we need to, let us forgive everyone who has wronged us. If necessary, let us make right with anyone who might be offended with us. Wherever you need to in your life—make right. Know this; as we pursue holiness, we are pursuing the *Holy* Spirit, we are pursuing revival.

And so we pray...

Lord, I bow my heart and bend my knee,
send revival, and start with me;
Pour out your Spirit in an unprecedented way;
May all who hear be saved today;
May all who are saved proclaim the Way;
Lord send revival and start with me.

Add some ink: *My thoughts and prayers on this day;*

_____

_____

_____

_____

DAY 13

Humility is Absolutely Necessary

*If My people who are called by My name will **humble** themselves, and pray and seek My face, and turn from their wicked ways, then I will hear from heaven, and will forgive their sin and heal their land.*

II CHRONICLES 7:14 NKJV

We know the prayer of 2 Chronicles well! It is a verse of hope when our land is hurting and broken. When our country is over-run by wicked people when the economy is crashing, when disease is rife when crime is out of control. This is the verse we go to. This is the verse that South Africans turned to in early 1994, when full scale civil war was threatening to tear the fabric of society ahead of the first democratic elections. They are the words of God, and they are words of life and hope. They are a great promise that we can stand on; God will hear us and He will heal our land…

There is however, a condition to note, it says; *"If My people who are called by My name would **humble** themselves…"* Humility is the key to unlocking the promise of healing in this scripture. It is a kingdom virtue of exceptional value and completely necessary as a precursor to revival.

For this is what the high and exalted One says—he who lives forever, whose name is holy: "I live in a high and holy place, but

*also with the one who is contrite and lowly in spirit, to **revive***
*the spirit of the lowly and to **revive** the heart of the contrite.*
ISAIAH 57:15 NIV

Who does God dwell with and who does He revive? The lowly and contrite; the humble. Revival is reserved for the humble. Humility is a rare virtue and easily overlooked or ignored in our day. Our world is not impressed with it, but it is sought, prized, and pursued by God. It has a magnetic-God quality. It attracts Him more than anything. He delights in it. He rewards it. He chooses it as His dwelling and place of revival.

"Has not my hand made all these things, and so they came into being?"
declares the Lord. "These are the ones I look on with favour: those who
*are **humble** and contrite in spirit, and who tremble at my word."*
ISAIAH 66:2 NIV

The great intercessor, Andrew Murray, wrote:

> Humility is not a thing we bring to God. It is also not a thing God
> gives to us. It is simply the realisation of what nothings we really
> are, when we truly see how God is everything, and when we clear
> out room in our hearts so that He can be everything for us.

Humility comes when we truly see how God is everything to us. As long as God is "something" and not "everything" we won't fully possess this virtue called humility. Revivalists have all had something in common, they all arrived at the place (albeit in different ways and circumstances) where God became everything to them. He was not just another *thing* in their lives. Having Him was not another objective... it was everything. His name, His glory, His desires, His mission, took absolute precedence over their names, their success, their desires, and their mission. That is humility.

Not to us, O Lord, not to us, but to your name goes all the glory for your unfailing love and faithfulness.
PSALM 115:1 NLT

Such was the heart of Cornelius in Acts chapter 10. He was a Roman, which meant that he was separate from the covenants and promises of God. Cornelius was also rich and powerful! He could have looked down with pride on Jews and lived a comfortable life, but he chose to seek God's face and pray and give generously to the Jews and to the poor. The result was God could not ignore his humble heart. He sent Peter to his house and poured out a wonderful revival on him and all his household.

God often chooses the humblest places and people for revival. In the early 1990s, He chose a small church in Toronto near the airport for an outpouring that would see millions coming through the doors. That small church became the number one tourist destination in Canada! He chose a wooden building in Azusa Street on the wrong side of town. It had sawdust on the floor and used two wooden shoe boxes as a pulpit. The leader of the revival, William Seymour, was the son of former slaves and would often put his head in those boxes and pray for hours every day. He was a man marked by humility.

Scripture describes Moses as the most humble man on earth (Numbers 12:3) and think of how God met with him... so that Moses' face beamed God's glory. But none of this should surprise us, because He also chose a manger as His place of birth. He chose Nazareth. He chose slaves in Egypt. He chose uneducated fishermen. He is attracted to humility.

But God has chosen the foolish things of the world to put to shame the wise, and God has chosen the weak things of the world to put to shame the things which are mighty; and the base things of the world and the things which are despised God has chosen, and the things which are not, to bring to nothing the things that are, that no flesh should glory in His presence.
I Corinthians 1:27-29 NKJV

As we pray for revival, let's remember that we are humbling ourselves. We are emptying ourselves of ourselves because we see God and the move of God in our generation as our everything. Nothing is more important or desirable to us, but that He would rend the heavens and come down, establish His kingdom and take His glory. And this is why when we pray for revival, we *bow our hearts and bend our knees...*

And so we pray...

Lord, I bow my heart and bend my knee,
send revival, and start with me;
Pour out your Spirit in an unprecedented way;
May all who hear be saved today;
May all who are saved proclaim the Way;
Lord send revival and start with me.

Add some ink: *My thoughts and prayers on this day;*

_____

_____

_____

_____

_____

DAY 14

A Riot of Joy

*All that He is He sees reflected fully and perfectly in the
countenance of His Son and in this He rejoices with infinite joy.*
JOHN PIPER

We have heard of repentance, tears, and confession as a result of God coming near, but what of the joy and freedom that is also seen? Revival is often a riot of joy. Revivals are often marked with intense laughter, belly's bursting with joy, shrieks of delight, and tears of those overwhelmed by freedom… true freedom.

If ever there was a need for a revival of joy it would be now! Think how serious we have become. Think about the faces on the bus or in the taxi. Have you ever looked at the people in the car next to you? Did you see them smiling? What about the queue at the bank or in the supermarket? Were people beaming with life and joy? Or were they surviving; head down, focused, determined, overwhelmed, burdened, angry, bitter, impartial, uncaring, or numb! A big *DO NOT DISTURB* sign above their heads.

Such is modern life. A smile is a rare thing. And joy is sparsely found. What about a revival of joy! What about some laughter from heaven? Let's remember, there are no tears in heaven only continual bliss and adoration and fullness of joy. When we pray for revival, we are asking for heaven to come to earth, so we can ask for and even expect joy to be part of revival.

David said of the Lord: "*In Your presence is **fullness of joy;** At Your right hand are pleasures forevermore*" (Psalms16:11 NKJV).

Fullness of Joy! In other words, the absolute maximum possible experience of joy is found in the presence of God.

"At your right hand are pleasures forevermore!" No greater pleasure will we ever have than to be with God. Once we have tasted the goodness of God—the absolute bliss of being near to Him we are ruined for anything else life could offer. Nothing else can ever come close.

To encounter Him is to encounter true rest, it is to arrive home and be released from every heavy burden of life. *"Come to me, all of you who are weary and carry heavy burdens, and I will give you rest"* (Matthew 11:28 NLT).

How many weary people can you think of that need an encounter with the joyous, burden-destroying, soul-satisfying Jesus of the Bible? When revival hit Samaria in Acts chapter 8 it says, *"and there was **great joy** in that city..."* I think our city could do with a bit of that!

Wherever Jesus went there was a trail of great joy. People healed, saved, and delivered. Could our God want us to be happy? I think so...

> *One thing have I asked of the Lord, that will I seek, inquire for, and [insistently] require: that I may dwell in the house of the Lord [in His presence] all the days of my life, to behold and gaze upon the beauty [the sweet attractiveness and the delightful loveliness] of the Lord and to meditate, consider, and inquire in His temple.*
> PSALM 27:4 AMPC

Step aside Bono, these are the words of someone who has found what he has been looking for. He just wants to gaze, behold, be

W. Samuel Sandeman

near, dwell—these are the words of a godly hedonist—he can't get enough of God.

Life is a search for pleasure. We are always looking for what makes us feel good, we buy what is desirable to our eyes, satisfying to our flesh, enjoyable to our senses, but as much as we can get in this world it seems the search never ends. There is a hole that cannot be filled. We know because like many before him and since, King Solomon tried and failed. He said,

> *Whatever my eyes desired I did not keep from them. I did not*
> *withhold my heart from any pleasure, for my heart rejoiced*
> *in all my labour… Then I looked on all the works that my*
> *hands had done and on the labour in which I had toiled;*
> *and indeed, all was vanity and grasping for the wind.*
> ECCLESIASTES 2:10-11 NKJV

'Grasping for the wind.' That is all we arrive at when we set our pleasure on anything but God. How many people are trapped in this 'grasping for the wind?' They are all around us every day! When we pray for revival, we are praying for their freedom. We are praying for our city to be released from the burdens of sin, sickness, Satan, and excessive stress… we are praying for the demise of the epidemic of daily depression. We are praying for a time of jubilant joy.

On the other hand, God himself is supremely joyful. He is happy with himself and takes pleasure in all that he does and all that He has made. Most of all, He takes pleasure in His Son, Jesus. He is the fountain of joy. Christ's invitation is for us, who are thirsty, to drink from his fountain of joy. The Bible calls it "joy in the Holy Spirit" (Romans 14:17). The Holy Spirit allows us to see what the Father sees: the face of Jesus. In his profound book, *"The Pleasures of God"* John Piper wrote:

From all eternity God beheld the panorama of his own perfections in the face of his Son. All that He is He sees reflected fully and perfectly in the countenance of His Son and in this He rejoices with infinite joy.

God is supremely joyful. That is good news! In fact, according to a more literal translation of 1 Timothy 1:11, the Christian Gospel is "the good news of the glory of the happy God." The word that is translated as "blessed" in this verse in most versions of the Bible is the Greek, "*makarios*"—also used in the beatitudes. "*Makarios*" means "happy" or "fortunate." Now, Jonathan Edwards wrote that the Holy Spirit is the manifestation of joy that the Father and Son have in their relationship with each other. When the Holy Spirit comes upon us, He invites us into that joyful relationship of pure love.

So, let's keep asking and let's keep seeking revival because it is going to be marvellous! It is going to be just what our city needs! It is what our churches need, what people need, what we need at this time: revival is a riot of joy!

And so we pray...

> *Lord, I bow my heart and bend my knee,*
> *send revival, and start with me;*
> *Pour out your Spirit in an unprecedented way;*
> *May all who hear be saved today;*
> *May all who are saved proclaim the Way;*
> *Lord send revival and start with me.*

Add some ink: *My thoughts and prayers on this day;*

_____

_____

_____

_____

_____

DAY 15

Liberty to Captives

Prayer is not overcoming God's reluctance
but laying hold of His willingness.
MARTIN LUTHER

I n his Gospel, Luke relates an amazing and beautiful incident in the ministry of Jesus:

'Now He was teaching in one of the synagogues on the Sabbath.
And behold, there was a woman who had a spirit of infirmity
eighteen years and was bent over and could in no way raise herself
up. But when Jesus saw her, He called her to Him and said to her,
"Woman, you are loosed from your infirmity." And He laid His
hands on her, and immediately she was made straight, and glorified
God. But the ruler of the synagogue answered with indignation,
because Jesus had healed on the Sabbath; and he said to the crowd,
"There are six days on which men ought to work; therefore,
come and be healed on them, and not on the Sabbath day."

The Lord then answered him and said, "Hypocrite! Does not each
one of you on the Sabbath loose his ox or donkey from the stall,
and lead it away to water it? So, ought not this woman, being a
daughter of Abraham, whom Satan has bound for eighteen years,
be loosed from this bond on the Sabbath?" And when He said these

W. Samuel Sandeman

things, all His adversaries were put to shame; and all the multitude
rejoiced for all the glorious things that were done by Him.'
LUKE 13:10-17 NKJV

Think about it... This woman was bent over for 18 years! Jesus said it was Satan who had bound her. He called it infirmity. Satan and infirmity; two things Jesus had to do something about! The Scripture said: *"When he saw her he called for her"*—he targeted her. This was while he was in the middle of preaching to a crowd in the synagogue. He saw *her*. He stopped what he was doing to free her from her bondage, her suffering, pain, and shame. She became his priority. He could not allow her bondage to go on any longer. Why? Because this is His mission. This is the reason He came. Jesus hates bondage in any form. Bondage is the work of Satan, and "for this reason did the Son of God come in the flesh: to destroy the works of the evil one" (1 John 3:8).

The book of Isaiah declares His mission: *'To proclaim liberty to the captives, and the opening of the prison to those who are bound."* (Isaiah 61:1 NKJV).

He came to open prisons. Proclaim liberty to captives. How many captives are there right now all around us? How many people are bound in prisons of shame, sickness, and sin? Bound in unforgiveness, hate, and even hurt. So many are bound in fear, insecurity, depression, and systems of slavery and abusive relationships. So many are bound in false religion and ideologies. I think of our addicts and I think of our prostitutes, our corporate greed, and our queues at the hospitals packed with systemic and chronic diseases; I think of our nightclubs and taverns packed to capacity. There are so many bound in so many different ways... so many are captive to Satan.

When we pray for revival, we are not just praying for liberty. We are praying for MASS liberty. We are praying for an all-out assault from heaven against ALL enemy strongholds. This is what happens in revival: scores of people are set free from every form of bondage you can imagine.

> *Now the Lord is the Spirit; and where the*
> *Spirit of the Lord is, there is liberty.*
> II Corinthians 3:17 NKJV

When the Spirit of the Lord comes, top on His agenda is liberty. All infirmities, addictions, wrong thinking, crutches, conditions, and emotions that keep people bound are targeted. It is mass liberation. It is every cell within the prison opening, heck, it is the prison walls tumbling down! It is people set free to be who they were called to be, no longer trapped and oppressed, but free. Can you imagine, liberty like this coming to our campuses, schools, our neighbourhoods, our city? Revival is liberty! Can you hear William Wallace shouting for freedom? That is the shout of heaven: *"Let my people go! That they may worship me!"*

This is what we are praying for!

Take heart in what Martin Luther said: *"Prayer is not overcoming God's reluctance but laying hold of His willingness."*

Jesus was willing to set that woman free. He was willing to cleanse the lepers. He cast out every demon. Let us lay hold of that willingness and pray for a revival that will bring liberty to us and all the captives around us.

W. Samuel Sandeman

And so we pray...

Lord, I bow my heart and bend my knee,
send revival, and start with me;
Pour out your Spirit in an unprecedented way;
May all who hear be saved today;
May all who are saved proclaim the Way;
Lord send revival and start with me.

Add some ink: *My thoughts and prayers on this day;*

_____

_____

_____

_____

_____

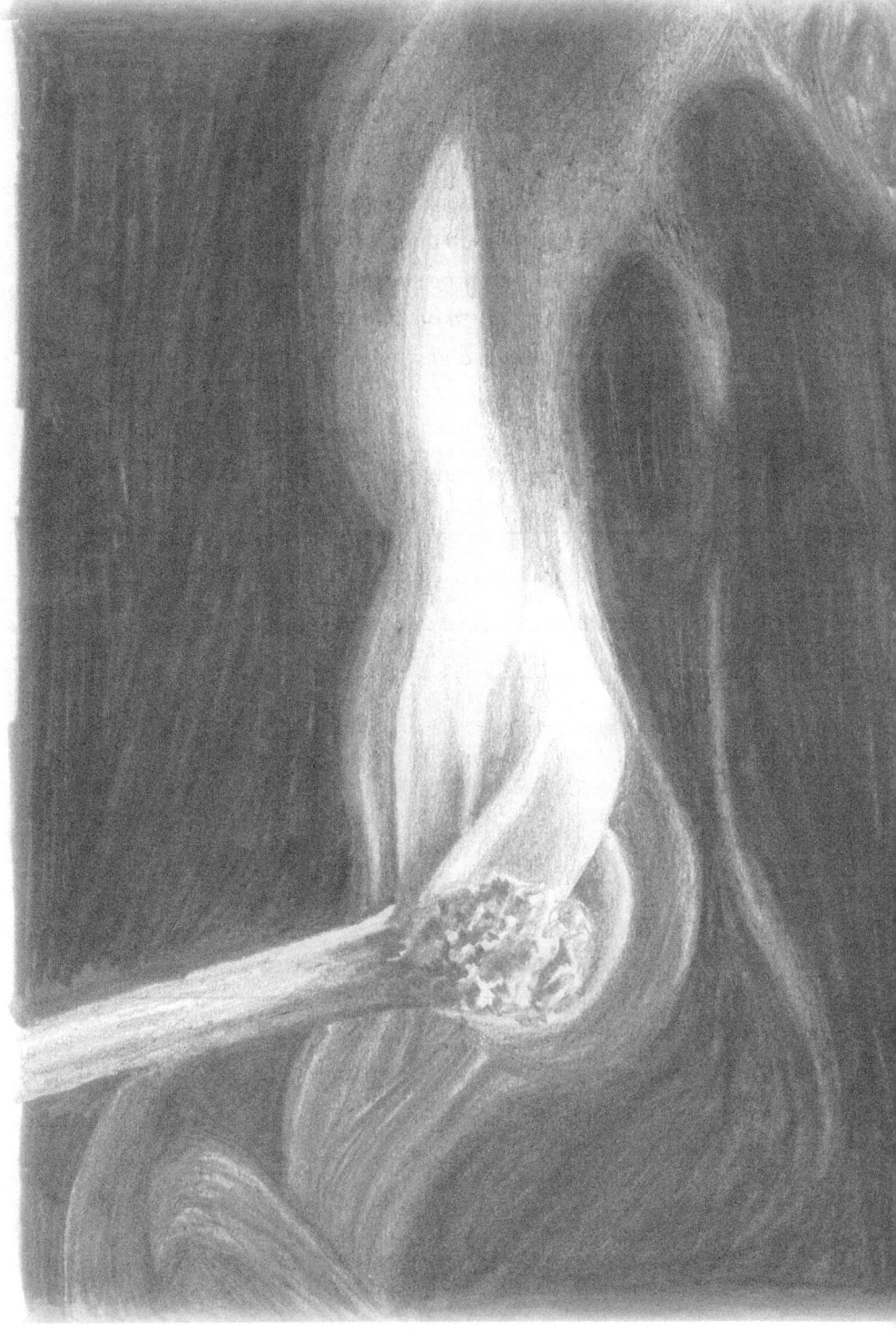

DAY 16

One Spark

*Her life was so radically changed that it became the talk of the town
and the news of this evident act of God's grace spread like wildfire.*
JONATHAN EDWARDS
(REVIVAL IN NORTHAMPTON, MASSACHUSETTS 1734)

All it takes is one spark to light a fire. Revival typically begins
with a spark—an event or a person who the Lord uses to
trigger the fire of revival.

The earliest example in the Gospels is the woman at the well
in John chapter 4. One encounter with Jesus was enough to set her
running into the town and gather a huge crowd. Have you ever
wondered how this woman managed to gather such a large crowd
in the middle of the day? Surely people were busy. They must have
had things to do. She wasn't an influential leader in the town. In all
probability, she was the opposite: someone who was looked down on
because of her personal life, which was a mess. Why would people
listen to this rejected woman who had to draw water when nobody
else was around? What made them down their tools, listen to her
and even follow her out the town? How could this *she* become the
effective messenger?

It was because she carried 'the spark.' She had the anointing and
it broke every yoke. She was instantly made free and her freedom
carried a captivating power. Power to influence an entire village:

So, there were many from the Samaritan village who became believers in Jesus because of the woman's testimony.
JOHN 4:39 TPT

In other words, there was no denying that something marvellous had happened to this woman—she was alive—and it was too attractive not to be a part of it. She was the spark that set the town on fire. And what an unlikely spark she was!

This was similar to what happened in the first Great Awakening in North America:

The American colonies were in a tragic spiritual decline and moral decadence ruled the day. The frontier areas had no churches, and they were lawless. There was a continual war with the indigenous peoples. Christianity was in a very low state. Believers were generally, lifeless, careless, and carnal. In Pennsylvania Rev. Samuel Blair stated: *"Christianity lay as it were dying, and ready to expire its last breath of life..."* It appeared to be a hopeless situation.

That was until the remnant of believers began to pray and ask God to move and save their friends and neighbours... and God heard those prayers. He always does. Saints, it is so important that we pray for the lost!

What happened next was Jonathan Edwards began to preach the Gospel and one young woman who was described as *"one of the greatest company keepers in the whole town"* gave her heart to Jesus. Her life was so radically changed that it became the talk of the town and news of this spread like wildfire. In the next six months, 25% of the population was converted to Christ. What a wildfire from just one spark! Again, a very unlikely spark.

In the year 1802 Yale university became the centre of a revival. All it took was two students who were overwhelmed with the conviction of their sins. In a short period of time, they came to faith

W. Samuel Sandeman

in Christ. This made a huge impact on the other students, it led to one-third of the student body committing to Christ. The revival then spread to other universities and there was a resurgence of faith that followed.

Can you imagine: only two students getting saved led to one-third of the whole student body committing their lives to Christ? Amazing! It sounds like the story of Jonathan and his armour bearer, does it not? These two were the spark that set the fire of revival to the whole campus. Can you imagine something like this happening on our university campuses? Is there not a need for this in our campuses today? I want you to know that when we pray for revival this is not a difficult thing for the Lord God to do.

Sometimes we can get bogged down with *how* revival might happen, or *how* much work will be needed, or what we need to do to get a whole campus or city to a meeting. We can get worried about *how* we can gather crowds. Sometimes the task looks overwhelmingly difficult, or just plain impossible. People are so busy with their lives and day-to-day tasks—what will make them stop and listen and hear the Gospel?

The answer: just one spark; an anointed spark; a spark on which God breathes His holy breath. Two unlikely women gathered two unlikely towns to salvation. Two unlikely students gathered a university to Christ. God knows how to draw crowds. His anointing breaks every yoke.

Revival is the power of God. It is the anointing of God. And God knows how to start a fire with just one spark. God is looking for a spark on which He can breathe to create holy fire. Let's pray for sparks to fly. Let's pray for the Lord to radically touch unlikely people and set them on fire like those women were. Let's share the Gospel every chance we get and every time we do let's pray that person becomes a spark. Who knows; one sermon could become the spark, one podcast, one song, one phone call—just one!

And so we pray...

> Lord, I bow my heart and bend my knee,
> send revival, and start with me;
> Pour out your Spirit in an unprecedented way;
> May all who hear be saved today;
> May all who are saved proclaim the Way;
> Lord send revival and start with me.

Add some ink: *My thoughts and prayers on this day;*

_____

_____

_____

_____

DAY 17

Ask!

Ask, and it will be given to you; seek, and you will find; knock,
and it will be opened to you. For everyone who asks receives, and
he who seeks finds, and to him who knocks, it will be opened.
MATTHEW 7:7-8 NKJV

In our world, it is rude to ask someone for a gift. We do not walk up to people and say, *'Please can I have a gift.'* Yet in the kingdom of God, we are invited to ask. Asking is a good thing. In fact, do not just ask, knock and seek as well! And not just for gifts, for **good** gifts.

In I Corinthians 12:31 we are told to *"…earnestly **desire** the best gifts…"*

And if you don't see any immediate response then keep on asking and seeking! How different from the world we live in! If we ask for something and don't get an answer we back off—in God's kingdom, we are invited to ramp it up.

In James 4:2 We are told that *we have not because we ask not.* And this is so true with revival!

Think about it: how many times in your life have you asked for revival? Well, hopefully, since you have been working through this book, you have been asking for revival. But before then, had you ever sought for it? I mean, have you really looked for revival? Do you ever remember losing something important and turning your house upside down to try and find it? That's the kind of seeking I'm talking about, that's the kind of seeking Jesus was talking about. Have we ever done that when it comes to revival? Have we ever launched an all-out pursuit like those mass searches we launch for missing persons? Are we not missing the person of the Holy Spirit?

What is the content of the asking we bring to heaven's door? Better jobs, better cars, money, clothes, things, a husband, a wife, good health, protection on the roads, righteous leaders, the economy to grow... don't get me wrong these are all good gifts that God does give, but could there be a better gift than God sending a revival to our church and city?

Remember revival is God pouring out His Spirit and that does not mean He pours out some impersonal energy source or power upon us—it means that the third person of the Trinity, being God the Holy Spirit, comes near. That is what revival is.

In Genesis 15:1 God came to Abram in a vision saying: *"Do not be afraid, Abram. I am your shield, your exceedingly great reward."*

I AM your exceedingly great reward! I AM the best gift or reward you could ever have. God is the best gift and this should be our biggest ask—and this is what we are asking for when we pray for revival.

I remember the day I asked my parents-in-law for their daughter's hand in marriage. I could have asked them for many things. They are such generous people they would give away just about anything they owned. Such is the family I married into. But I asked for the best they had, I asked for the person of their daughter.

Our Father in heaven is also so generous He too would give us so many things we could ever ask for, but when we ask for the person of the Holy Spirit we are asking for the best and most that He can give and in the process, we show Him the greatest honour and love.

I think of the words to a popular song; *'we don't want blessings we want you.'*

Would we take heaven if God wasn't there? God offered Moses the promised land, but Moses said; *'I don't want it if your Spirit does not go with us.'* (Exodus 33:15) Moses wanted God's Spirit more than anything the world could offer him—even a land of promise.

Psalm 42:2 agrees: *"My soul thirsts for God, for the living God. When can I go and meet with God?"*

What do our souls thirst for? What do we long for? Dream about? Could there be anything better than revival? Psalm 42 is a revival prayer: *'my soul thirsts for God, for the living God—when will you rend the heavens and come down?'*

Let us make asking for the Holy Spirit our number one ask. Let's be clear about what we want—we want God the Holy Spirit!

He can come like a mighty rushing wind,
He can come in the power of cleansing conviction,
He can come like the dew in the morning,
He can come like a river of joy,
He can come in tongues of fire or like a dove,
It doesn't matter; just let Him come!

And let us be ready to receive and welcome Him however He comes. Jesus said: *"For everyone who asks receives, and he who seeks finds, and to him who knocks it will be opened..."* Luke 11:10 NKJV.

And so we pray...

Lord, I bow my heart and bend my knee,
send revival, and start with me;
Pour out your Spirit in an unprecedented way;
May all who hear be saved today;
May all who are saved proclaim the Way;
Lord send revival and start with me.

Add some ink: *My thoughts and prayers on this day;*

_____

_____

_____

_____

_____

W. Samuel Sandeman

DAY 18

Children and Revival

And afterward, I will pour out my Spirit on all people.
Your sons and daughters will prophesy, your old men will
dream dreams, your young men will see visions.
JOEL 2:28 NIV

Matthew records in his Gospel account that Jesus said; *"Let the little children come to me, and do not hinder them, for the kingdom of heaven belongs to such as these." When He had placed His hands on them, he went on from there"* (Matthew 19:14-15 NIV).

It may surprise you to hear that children have always had a part in revivals. They are not on the side-lines or an afterthought in God's agenda to renew people. Many times in history, they have been the spark that sets the revival going—the 'first receivers', who then bring their families to the Lord.

When revival comes our sons and daughters begin to prophesy and see visions. Sometimes they sing songs never heard before and when questioned they say they heard angels singing the songs.

No wonder Jesus said, *"Truly I tell you, unless you change and become like little children, you will never enter the kingdom of heaven"* (Matthew 18:3 NIV).

Children have a wonderful ability to believe and receive. God called Samuel when he was just a young Boy—and Samuel heard. Young Samuel might not have understood at first, but once coached he was ready to hear more and God downloaded to a little boy what was to become of the nation of Israel. He gave His plan to a child!

Charles Finney, the famous revivalist, would often use school halls to preach in when traveling. At one particular school he preached in the evening to a small group of bored people who had come to listen, but nothing happened. However, the next day when the children arrived for classes in the same school the Holy Spirit swept through the classrooms, and children began to weep randomly, first one, then another until it was almost all of them. One child exclaimed, 'I fear for my soul!' Another cried, "I'm afraid of hell" this happened in multiple classrooms all at the same time. The teachers met in the hallways perplexed not knowing what to do as their pupils were overcome in repentance. The school principal, knowing Mr. Finney had held a meeting the night before, asked for Finney to come back and preach to the children. When he did, many children gave their lives to Christ that day. Needless to say, that evening the school meetings were packed with the parents all wanting to know what happened to their children… and the revival was on!

Those first adults sat under Finney's preaching and did not react. They were cold and dead. I think of the account in Mark Chapter 6:5, where it records, *"Jesus could not do any miracles in his hometown of Nazareth, except lay his hands on a few sick people and heal them and He was amazed at their lack of faith."*

Unbelief can be a roadblock to revival. So, I like to think that God took Finney's sermon and pushed pause on it, leaving the words hanging magically in the rooms of the school until a more receptive people arrived. When the children came in God just pushed play and the Word of God was back in motion.

Schools are often hotbeds for revivals. Just a few years ago a beautiful revival came to a Christian school in Limpopo South Africa. The principal said:

Students are constantly being moved to tears, they are prophesying over one another, they are getting visions, witnessing angels, being delivered and healed and many are being physically touched by God in such a way that they are shaking under the presence... There has been incredible hunger and passion among the vast majority of our students, so that at the slightest nudge they can easily spend three hours in worship.

In Azusa Street revival children were regular in attendance, participating, receiving, singing, and even prophesying and laying hands on the sick. Babies would not cry or disturb the meetings—they were often unusually quiet and receptive as God's presence filled the room tangibly and even visibly in the form of a cloud. One mother would bring her three-year-old daughter who would always go and lie under the pulpit at some points being in a playful mood she would be seen trying to gather the thick mist of God's shekinah glory into her arms.

As we pray for revival today, let us pray for God to pour out His Spirit on all our children. Let them be at the centre of the now revival. Let us pray our children have dreams and visions, angelic encounters, and hear God calling them as Samuel did. I think about all the temptations and challenges this young generation are facing—it is like an all-out assault on them from the enemy—so let us pray for an all-out assault from heaven upon them now!

And so we pray...

Lord, I bow my heart and bend my knee,
send revival, and start with me;
Pour out your Spirit in an unprecedented way;
May all who hear be saved today;
May all who are saved proclaim the Way;
Lord send revival and start with me.

Add some ink: *My thoughts and prayers on this day;*

_____

_____

_____

_____

_____

DAY 19

What Do You Want?

*God instituted prayer in order to lend to His
creatures the dignity of causality."*
BLAISE PASCAL

First words are important words, especially if we are looking at the life of Jesus and especially if we are looking at the Gospel of John. John's choice of words is so precise and poetic that when you ponder them you have to conclude that only God could have inspired them and their timing.

Surprisingly Jesus's first words in the Gospel of John are not about Him, or even His Father or the kingdom. At first glance, they can seem so insignificant and random that you might not even see anything profound in them, but they are loaded with power and invitation.

They are the words: "What do you want?"

In learning isiZulu, I learned the wrong way to ask for something. I said *'ngifuna'*, which translated means *I want*. It's not polite nor honouring to say that. It is demanding; definitely not the right choice of words when asking for a cup of tea. It is seen as pushy to say *ngifuna*. Much better to use the word *ngicela* which is far more polite; "please may I have..." I can fully understand that because I grew up learning that: *I want* doesn't get, because to say *'I want'* is rude.

However, in the kingdom "I want" gets. We are invited to have a big want and a big ask.

Jesus first words in John are: *What do you want?*

And then, He continued to use them in His ministry. He asked blind Bartimaeus 'What do you want?'

He asked lepers, 'What do you want?' Why ask such a silly question? Wasn't it obvious what they needed? Surely Jesus knew? Why ask them?

And why do we have to even express our needs and wants when Matthew 6:8 says, *"Your Father knows what you need before you ask Him."* So why do we still have to ask?

This is so important to understand, especially as we position ourselves to intercede for revival!

Blaise Pascal—the brilliant 17th century scientist, theologian and philosopher—said, *"God instituted prayer in order to lend to His creatures the dignity of causality."* In other words, God has not subjected us to fatalism, but instead, He has given us a voice, an opinion, position, authority, and an opportunity to influence the outcome of life and history through communicating our needs, desires, and wants to Him. We get to play apart.

What do you want?

He dignifies the whole human race with just those simple words! They show that He cares for our opinion and our desires—they are valid, and we matter.

What do you want?

W. Samuel Sandeman

I respect you, come up a level, and talk with me. I don't just want to rule over you or decide it all as though you are some worm in need of a totalitarian ruler.

What do you want?

Let's work together. Let's be partners. Give me your opinion. Let me hear how you see it.

What do you want?

In the kingdom *I want*, gets. So, what *do* we want? Moses and Elijah said; *'I want to see your glory.'*

Blind Bartimaeus asked for eyesight. Jairus asked for his daughter's life. The list goes on...

So, let's be clear about what we want.

How many souls do we want? What kind of miracles do we want? What do we want to see in our churches? Do we want to see visions? Do we want understanding or wisdom? Do we want to encounter His love? Do we want peace and joy? What gifts of the Spirit do we want? What sort of transformation do we want to see in our city when revival comes? Do you want to see God's glory? Let's go up to the level He has invited us, let's step into our role and authority, and let's put forth the best, most kingdom-soaked *wants* we can... because He invited us and in the kingdom of God, *I want* gets.

As we pray for revival let's be clear, specific, bold, and smart about what we want. Go on, you can do it, tell your Father in heaven what you want to see.

And so we pray...

Lord, I bow my heart and bend my knee,
send revival, and start with me;
Pour out your Spirit in an unprecedented way;
May all who hear be saved today;
May all who are saved proclaim the Way;
Lord send revival and start with me.

Add some ink: *My thoughts and prayers on this day;*

_____

_____

_____

_____

W. Samuel Sandeman

DAY 20

Glory

*It was as if a cloud or dense fog filled the church. In that service,
everyone who didn't have the baptism was baptised, and
everyone who was lost or backslidden got right with God.*
KENNETH HAGIN

When considering the magnitude of God's glory Solomon asked the question:

*But will God really live on earth? Why, even the highest heavens
cannot contain you. How much less this temple I have built!*
1 KINGS 8:27 NLT

And what a good point! God's glory cannot be contained; it is infinite in every way. Earth and everything in it is just so finite. Will God really live on earth? The answer to Solomon from God himself was an emphatic 'Yes!' He flooded Solomon's temple with His glory which spilled over into the nation of Israel, bringing peace and unparalleled prosperity. God wills to live on earth and He wills that all the earth will be overflowing with His glory.

*… but truly, as I live, all the earth shall be
filled with the glory of the LORD.*
NUMBERS 14:21 NKJV

I love the certainty and determination of this statement; *"TRULY, AS I LIVE, all the earth shall be filled with the glory of the LORD ."* heaven is where God's glory dwells; the heavens, we are told in the Psalms, proclaim His glory and as He lives, He wants the earth to be filled with His glory too.

> *The earth **will be** filled with the knowledge of the glory of the Lord, as the waters cover the sea.*
> HABAKKUK 2:14.

This scripture shows the passion of God for His glory to be known. As we move into the time of the latter rains, more Christians are speaking this verse. His passion is welling up in the saints of God through the Spirit of God in these last days and fuelling what I think is the greatest prayer movement ever seen. Truly we want to see His glory fill the earth!

> *For from the rising of the sun, even to its going down, My name shall be great among the nations.*
> MALACHI 1:11NKJV

Did you get that? God has an agenda for the earth; He wants to flood it with His glory. He flooded the temple that Solomon built such that the priests could not enter. He flooded the tabernacle that Moses built. And He hasn't stopped filling lives, buildings, and meetings with His glory. He has more plans to fill more!

When we are praying for revival, we are praying for our homes, churches, neighbourhoods, cities, and hearts to be filled with His glory. But what does that mean? And what does that look like?

The word 'glory' is translated as: *"the weight, the substance, the worth, the brilliance, the splendour, or the radiant beauty of God."* Meditate on that for a while.

When Moses cried, *'I want to see your glory,'* he was saying I want to see your radiant beauty, your brilliance, your worth... AND he wasn't denied! Why? because God wants to fill the earth with His glory. In 1677, Henry Scougal wrote in *The Life of God in the Soul of Man; "The worth and excellency of a soul is to be measured in the object of its love."* What is the object of God's greatest love? We see from Scripture that this object of great love is Himself in the form of His Son, Jesus. The object of Jesus' greatest love is His heavenly Father. Their mutual passion is for the glory of God. This is great news, because it tells us that God **wants** His glory to be seen and known.

When babies are born, when the sun sets over the ocean in a thousand pastel colours, when the stars shine, and when the world of waterfalls and snow-capped peaks glow in colours and majesty that assaults and overloads our senses—we catch a glimpse of the glory of God in creation. Likewise, when the blind see again, when the lame walk, the lost come home, the captives are set free—we catch a glimpse of the glory of God in operation. When we see kindness and generosity, self-sacrificing love, genuine friendship, and care—we catch a glimpse of the glory of God in mankind.

To pray for God's glory is to pray that our world will be filled with His beauty, His radiance, and worth. It is to pray that He would come near and everything that has been broken or tainted by sin will be corrected and re-aligned with His perfect will.

Kenneth Hagin spoke about the day God's glory filled his church, saying,

It was as if a cloud or dense fog filled the church. In that service, everyone who didn't have the baptism was baptised, and everyone

who was lost or backslidden got right with God. Miracles broke
out in the audience without anyone praying for them.

Yes, that is the glory of God! Everything that has been broken or tainted—corrected and re-aligned with His good pleasing and perfect will. No wonder David said, *"LORD, I have loved the habitation of Your house, the place where Your glory dwells"* (Psalms26:8 NKJV).

The place where His glory dwells is the place of perfection and completeness. It is heaven on earth. And this is what we are to pray for: *"Thy kingdom come Thy will be done on earth as it is in heaven"*

Revival is God's glory coming to town, and don't we want that!

And so we pray...

Lord, I bow my heart and bend my knee,
send revival, and start with me;
Pour out your Spirit in an unprecedented way;
May all who hear be saved today;
May all who are saved proclaim the Way;
Lord send revival and start with me.

Add some ink: *My thoughts and prayers on this day;*

_____
_____
_____
_____
_____

W. Samuel Sandeman

DAY 21

P.U.S.H.

*I have pastored only three churches in my more than
sixty years of ministry. We had revival in every one. And
not one of them came as a result of my preaching.*
SIDLOW BAXTER

Twenty-one days of praying for revival. I think of Daniel setting
his face to fast and pray and receiving a breakthrough after 21
days. What I find most interesting is that there is no indication that
Daniel knew it was going to take 21 days before the angel Gabriel
broke through the principalities to bring word and vision to him. I
wonder how long he would have gone? He didn't know the answer
would come on day 21. I also wonder what would have happened
if he gave up on day 15 or 19, thinking that maybe his prayer didn't
work. Would he still have seen the results of his prayer?

This is similar to the disciples in the Upper Room. Jesus said:

*Behold, I send the Promise of My Father upon you; but tarry in the
city of Jerusalem until you are endued with power from on high.*
LUKE 24:49 NKJV

He didn't say how long they were to wait and He didn't tell them
what the answer would look like. Both Daniel and the early disciples
were praying until… They didn't fully know what the answer would
be or how long it would take. Daniel's came in 21 days, the disciples

tarried 10 days; they were not on a prayer and fasting program with key points, bible readings and meal plans to follow each day. They were just there praying until...

This is where we get the acronym: **P.U.S.H.** = Pray Until Something Happens.

English preacher Sidlow Baxter, when he was eighty-five years of age, said:

> I have pastored only three churches in my more than sixty years of ministry. We had revival in every one. And not one of them came as a result of my preaching. They came as a result of the membership entering into a covenant to **PRAY UNTIL** revival came. And it did come, every time.

They prayed until—until revival came. They did not know when it would or how it would, they just committed until. He called it a 'covenant of prayer'. That is a word we don't hear too often. Covenant—it is the highest commitment. It's marriage, it's for better or worse, come what may this is where you will find me on my knees until... until the answer comes and whatever shape it comes in.

The Faith Mission that sent Duncan Campbell also started with a covenant to pray...

> For ten days, people had gathered to seek God each evening after work, sometimes continuing all night until dawn. 'A day came... when the very room was shaken, as in the days of the early church and we were filled with the Holy Spirit, with joy unspeakable and full of glory.

They prayed until... until the room was shaken and until the Holy Spirit was given—they prayed until.

    W. Samuel Sandeman

There is something about result-orientated prayer i.e. praying until—it's just so biblical and so effective! It's how our Lord taught and inspired us to pray. It is different from praying for the sake of praying. You know, that religious clock-in, clock-out; *"I hope I said the right words, I'm sure God will do something with what I said or what I asked for, but if it happens or not I'm ok."*

That is not praying until. That is a fruitless exercise and something like spiritual tourism. Look and leave and have nothing to show except a t-shirt.

Praying until is… praying for results. It's what is needed if we are to see revival sweep our land and fill our churches.

We have spoken of some of the wonderful results of praying for revival: souls being saved, healings, mass deliverance, etc. But they don't just stop there, after the second great awakening there was also a radical reformation of society that followed the revival:

Christians became leaders in many social concerns such as education, prison reform, women's rights, child labour was stopped, the modern missionary movement was birthed (taking the Gospel to millions in foreign nations), Sunday Schools were started for children, and the Abolitionist movement put an end to slavery… the list goes on. Such remarkable results. Beyond the walls of the church, into society, into the business world, into government, into the laws and fabric of society.

As we continue with our covenant of prayer, let's be result orientated in our prayers. That is: having the heart to pray until— until we see the results we want. We are not participating in a spiritual exercise. We are praying for results and looking for them each day just as Elijah's servant was sent looking for answers to the prayers he was praying for rain (1 Kings 18).

So, let us not pray for the sake of praying, but for the sake of souls, for the sake of the sick and the captives, for the sake of society and its transformation. These are the results of revival, the results of praying until.

And so we pray...

> Lord, I bow my heart and bend my knee,
> send revival, and start with me;
> Pour out your Spirit in an unprecedented way;
> May all who hear be saved today;
> May all who are saved proclaim the Way;
> Lord send revival and start with me.

Add some ink: *My thoughts and prayers on this day;*

_____

_____

_____

_____

DAY 22

Witnesses

And with great power, the apostles gave witness
to the resurrection of the Lord Jesus...
ACTS 4:33

Final words, like first words, are important words. If we have the liberty of knowing when we are leaving this world, we are known for gathering loved ones and sharing final blessings as Isaac or Jacob did. Sometimes we declare our love for those closest to us or we give final important instructions for those who need them—these are our final words.

When it comes to Jesus most of us think His last words were; *"it is finished"* His statement of triumph on the cross. But those were not exactly His last words, three days later He rose from the dead and then spent 40 days with His disciples sharing many more words with them. They spoke about the kingdom and because Jesus was so real and relational it is recorded that He shared many meals with them as well. Food, friends, and kingdom talk, that's how Jesus rolled—what a glorious 40 days!

But then His day of ascension came and knowing He was going to leave He gave His final words; instructions which set the modus operandi for the church age...

But you shall receive power when the Holy Spirit has come
upon you, and you shall be witnesses to Me in Jerusalem, and
in all Judea and Samaria, and to the end of the earth.
ACTS 1:8 NKJV

A prophecy over their lives, a declaration of a certain future; *"YOU will be my witnesses"*—they sound to me like the words of a master who has successfully finished His work and is certain of the outcome. He might as well have said *"it is finished"* again. At the cross, He finished His work with sin, Satan, and death, but His work with His disciples was not yet done until this moment. They were not yet witnesses.

Witnesses. That's who they were called and trained to be. It's also what we are called to be. It sounds easy enough, but actually, it's a nearly impossible job. The word "Witness" is the Greek word *"martus"*. It is pronounced *"mar'toos"*. This is where we get our word *"martyr."* It implies death to self, but being alive to Christ. In other words: If you get me you get Christ. The apostle Paul described such a life in his second letter to the church in Corinth:

For Christ's love compels us, because we are convinced that
one died for all, and therefore all died. And he died for all,
that those who live should no longer live for themselves
but for him who died for them and was raised again.
2 CORINTHIANS 5:14-15 NIV

Now those are the words of a true witness; *"Christ's love compels us".* The word *‹compel›* has military connotations i.e. I am under the control of God's love. I live no longer for myself, but for Him and His great commission.

How do we live like that? Often, we are not controlled by the love of Christ and so often not devoted to the great commission. We lack a heart for the lost and we lack the words to share with them, we fear man, we do not want to be rejected, we never seem to find the right moment to share the Gospel with people, we don't walk with the revelation of heaven and hell being just a breath away and so we are not exactly witnesses. And neither were they; exactly… something still had to be done. They needed the power of the Holy Spirit to come upon them before they could be witnesses. And so do we.

When we pray for revival, we have been praying: *"May all who hear be saved today, may all who are saved proclaim the way."*

One of the most prevalent signs of a revival is the ease at which the Gospel not only pours forth in power from the pulpit, but also from the witness of everyday believers who fill the pews. When the Holy Spirit comes, He empowers us all to be what we are called to be… witnesses. This is how we know revival has come, we become controlled by the love of Christ and we live not for ourselves but for Him. And wherever we go, we witness. This pattern is borne out in the book of Acts:

And with great power, the apostles gave witness to the resurrection of the Lord Jesus. And great grace was upon them all.
ACTS 4:33 NKJV

That great grace that was upon them all, was the power of the Spirit enabling them to share Jesus effectively with their world. How we need that great grace!

Imagine a revival where we are all effective witnesses. Where we are not relying on pulpits, but everyday places become turning points for the lost. Imagine a revival where each one of us is empowered by the Spirit to share Jesus as naturally as we breathe.

Let's come honestly before the Lord and confess our weakness and our inadequacy of being witnesses, and let's agree; that is not who we want to be, and let's ask for the power of the Spirit to come on us so that we can be witnesses like they were.

And so we pray...

Lord, I bow my heart and bend my knee,
send revival, and start with me;
Pour out your Spirit in an unprecedented way;
May all who hear be saved today;
May all who are saved proclaim the Way;
Lord send revival and start with me.

Add some ink: *My thoughts and prayers on this day;*

_____
_____
_____
_____
_____

DAY 23

Revival & Mission

And this gospel of the kingdom will be preached in all the world as a witness to all the nations, and then the end will come.
MATTHEW 24:14 NKJV

There is so much talk about the end times. You could say we are a generation obsessed with the end of the age. But Jesus said, *"This Gospel of the kingdom will be preached in ALL the world as a witness to ALL the nations, and then the end will come."*

There is clearly a task to be done before the end will come. Why we spend our time looking for blood moons and antichrists and not for the reports of advancing missions is a mystery. As it stands just over three billion people on the planet are categorised as "unreached." Meaning they don't have a large enough evangelical church within their culture and language that could possibly share the Gospel with them. Right now, there are three billion lives; men, women, and children who are living in cultures where they might never hear the Gospel at all.

Often, we forget this because we drive down the street and see church buildings. We go to church. Most of the people we know got to church. Christianity is part of our culture in many ways. When you live in a blue world it is hard to imagine a yellow world and much harder to actually care enough to visit and invest in it especially if you are content with the colour of your world.

Looking through church history we see that there are two engines that typically drive the church out of its comfort and apathy and into the nations preaching the Gospel and planting churches as it should be. They are the engines of persecution and revival.

In the book of Acts, we see revival thrust the disciples out of the upper room and into the streets of Jerusalem, proclaiming the Gospel with everyone they could. However, for some reason, they still did not venture across cultural borders to share it with the Gentiles. That was until persecution came.

Persecution thrust them into the nations and we know in Antioch a great number of the Gentiles received the Gospel and a beautiful cross-cultural missional headquarters was established.

Revival and persecution. Two engines that get the church moving. I think of the words of David in Psalm 23 *"Your rod and staff they comfort me…"* the rod is discipline; the staff is grace. Discipline and grace. Persecution and revival.

I think we have a choice in the matter. As Paul wrote to the Corinthian church:

What do you want? Shall I come to you with a rod, or in love…?
I Corinthians 4:21 NKJV

I think all of us would prefer the engine of revival over that of persecution. *'Give us the staff and save us the rod!'* Revival is what the church needs if we are to get the job done. It won't be some clever missions program—though we need these programmes, rather it must be God touching lives and breaking hearts for nations and people groups, compelling people to go, declaring *'woe is me if I do not preach the Gospel!'*

I think of a few young men and women I have had the privilege of meeting who are burning for foreign nations. But they are too few. I wonder How many more are sitting with buried callings to nations and need the fire of God's spirit to activate and thrust them forth. Imagine a global revival that results in workers being thrust out from every corner of the world. We could get the job done and the end could come.

When we look at past revivals, we see something similar in most of them—they birthed missions, they thrust people to nations, they empowered people to be witnesses.

Revival leads to missions and revival is for missions. *'You will receive power when the Holy Spirit comes upon you, and you will be my witnesses... to the ends of the earth.'* The Holy Spirit is not only for personal comfort—though He touches us in incredible ways. He is there for the enriching of the nations with the treasure of the Gospel and that happens when He comes in power and turns us into witnesses.

So let us be clear; we pray for revival because we need to be better witnesses. We pray for revival because we need the Lord of the harvest to thrust workers into the harvest fields. We pray for revival because we care about the nations and 3 billion unreached people.

And so we pray...

Lord, I bow my heart and bend my knee,
send revival, and start with me;
Pour out your Spirit in an unprecedented way;
May all who hear be saved today;
May all who are saved proclaim the Way;
Lord send revival and start with me.

Add some ink: *My thoughts and prayers on this day;*

_____

_____

_____

_____

_____

DAY 24

Prize of Nations

*Again, the devil took him to a very high mountain and showed
him all the kingdoms of the world and their splendour. 'All
this I will give you,'" he said, "if you will bow down and
worship me." Jesus said to him, "Away from me, Satan! For it
is written: 'Worship the Lord your God and serve him only.*
MATTHEW 4:8-10 NIV

Satan doesn't tempt us with things that we are not interested
in. *All the kingdoms of the world and their splendour*"—that was
exactly what Jesus had come for. He wanted all the kingdoms
and their splendour in eternity with Him forever. This to Him is
the prize of earth. The things He desires and seeks… souls from
every tribe and tongue, plus all the unique and amazing gifts that
humanity shines with.

We must know that God loves humanity. He enjoys us. He
wants to be with us, hang out with us. He wants to adopt us and
call us family. He wants our opinions and He even respects our will
and decisions. People are His prize. He so loved the world that He
sent His Son to get the world. And here Jesus is being offered the
world, by the god of this world, Satan.

However, Father God had already offered Him the world in
Psalm 2:84: *"Ask of me and I will make the nations your inheritance, the
ends of the earth your possession…"*

Two offers from two very different sources. Satan's offer would be quick and seemingly easier than the cross, but it would last only a moment and then expire in a cloud of death and destruction just as so many people have experienced when it comes to Satan's promises. Instead, He took His Father's offer which would see Him go through the cross, and though it took much longer and was more painful to realise, it was full of life eternal.

The Revelation declares a day where Jesus gets what He paid for; it says:

Then the seventh angel sounded: And there were loud voices in heaven, saying, 'The kingdoms of this world have become the kingdoms of our Lord and of His Christ, and He shall reign forever and ever!'
REVELATION 11:15 NKJV

In the end, Jesus is victorious and the kingdoms of the world become His and He reigns forever and ever. When you come close to Jesus or He comes close to us, it's hard not to see and feel His passion for this purpose of having all the people of the world. It seems like the closer you get to Him or the closer He gets to you the more you catch it and become one with it.

John G Lake records how He went through a personal revival when the Holy Spirit came upon him. He said the following: *"A love for mankind such as I had never comprehended took possession of my life. Yea a soul yearning to see men saved, so deep, at times heartrending, until in anguish of soul I was compelled to abandon my business and turn all my attention to bringing men to the feet of Jesus..."*

It seems that the Lord's passion is contagious. And when we have it, we know revival has come to our hearts!

In the early 1700s, the Moravians that settled in Herrnhut Germany were a devout community of believers who had a

W. Samuel Sandeman

revelation of the power and purpose of prayer. They began to pray in extraordinary ways for God's mission to be fulfilled; that the kingdoms of the world would become Christs.

They called it the 'Hourly Intercession,' where relays of 24 men and 24 women, prayed without ceasing—that's 24/7/365—and they did not stop for 100 years! Prayer of that kind has only one result—revival! God sent revival to that community, and many would travel there from all over the world to experience a fresh touch from God.

My question is: was it the prayer that brought revival? Or was it the prayer for nations that brought revival? I believe it was the latter. The Holy Spirit was given for a purpose. To empower us to be witnesses, so that Jesus could have His prize of nations. When we align with that purpose and pray according to that purpose, we can be sure He—The Holy Spirit—will come.

And how He came on that community! As they prayed for nations, He came near and as He came near, they caught His passion—they became supernaturally passionate about what Jesus is passionate about, they were set on fire for nations!

From that one small village community in Herrnhut, more than one hundred missionaries went out in twenty-five years all over Europe and to places as far as the West Indies, the Arctic, the Far East, South America, and even South Africa. That is what happens when revival comes, God's purpose of reaching nations is fulfilled.

What do we learn from this? Firstly, Christ will have His nations. Secondly, when we pray according to this purpose, the Holy Spirit comes, we catch His passion and the job gets done. Prayer comes before heart; heart always comes before mission. No prayer, no heart; no heart, no mission. So, let's pray that He starts with our hearts and kindles in us a passion for what He is passionate about... nations!

And so we pray...

Lord, I bow my heart and bend my knee,
send revival, and start with me;
Pour out your Spirit in an unprecedented way;
May all who hear be saved today;
May all who are saved proclaim the Way;
Lord send revival and start with me.

Add some ink: *My thoughts and prayers on this day;*

_____

_____

_____

_____

_____

DAY 25

Ultimate Price for the Ultimate Prize

Looking unto Jesus, the author and finisher of our faith, who
for the joy that was set before Him endured the cross...
HEBREWS 12:2 NKJV

Jesus endured the cross because there was joy on the other side. What was that joy? I'm sure it was many things, especially the joy of pleasing His Father and accomplishing the Father's will for His life. However, there was also the joy of humanity saved from death and destruction, people (you and me!) able to enter eternal life and be with Him for all eternity. This was <u>also</u> the joy set before Him.

Jesus endured the cross so He could have His prize of nations. This means people, individuals like you, me and your neighbour, alive and well in eternity! To Him, the salvation of mankind was worth the pain, the shame, and all the suffering. What a lover of people this Saviour is! What does He see in mankind that we do not? He has no preference of colour or creed. He receives little children and even those who have lived rotten lives, who if in breathing their last they come to repentance, He accepts them all the same.

He said, *"For what will it profit a man if he gains the whole world, and loses his own soul?"* (Mark 8:36 NKJV).

Jesus was trying to help us understand our worth. Don't you see how valuable YOU are? Souls to Him are of infinite value and importance. To Him, we are worth the agony of the cross. We are, in

His eyes, worth suffering for. What does He see in us? What makes us so worth the sacrifice? He didn't go on such a rescue mission for the angels that fell from heaven. What value or use could we possibly be to Him?

The answer is because, unlike the angels, we carry His Image. We are made in *Imago Dei*, or *"the image of God."* We are made in His image and in His likeness. We carry value not because of what we do, but because of who we are and who we represent. We represent God in creation. We are valued not for our performance or for what we could do or bring, but because of our identity. We are meant to be the reflection of God's glory on earth as we are made in the image and likeness of God. This must not be lost but found and redeemed.

This is why He can look at the nations and have compassion on them, even while they rage against Him. He looks into cultures and He sees His image, He sees value. Something worth dying for. What do we see when we look at crowds and queues and cultures and ethnicities? Do we see what He sees—do we see value?

Love for humanity and a care for salvation is an expression of our love for God and a sign that revival has come to our hearts. When revival comes, we become full of God; we see what Christ sees and value what Christ values. In revival, people suddenly become precious to us. That is the work of God's Holy Spirit in us.

Two young Moravians who experienced the revival in Herrnhut in the early 1700s were filled with His Spirit and began to see the true value of souls. They heard of an island in the West Indies where an atheist British landowner owned between 2,000 and 3,000 slaves. The landowner was known for his hatred of religion and had even been heard to say that he would never allow a preacher or clergyman to stay on his island. The situation was that of thousands of slaves werec brought to an island and there to live and die without ever hearing of Christ. The precious *Imago Dei* would be lost.

So those two young Germans in their twenties decided to go, and if need be, become slaves that they might work among the slaves and in the process share the Gospel with them. The story is told that as they boarded a ship to what could be hardship and suffering they said these famous words to all those who had gathered to say goodbye; *"May the Lamb that was slain receive the reward of His suffering."*

They saw what Christ saw, they valued what Christ valued. They paid the ultimate price for the ultimate prize and their actions resulted in many others sowing their lives into foreign fields to search and redeem the lost image of God.

As we pray for revival, we are asking God to shift something in us so that we can see what He sees in people and that we too will spend ourselves freely so that the Lamb will receive the reward of his suffering. Let's pray that as we go about our day, we would see value in people and be empowered to be witnesses.

And so we pray...

Lord, I bow my heart and bend my knee,
send revival, and start with me;
Pour out your Spirit in an unprecedented way;
May all who hear be saved today;
May all who are saved proclaim the Way;
Lord send revival and start with me.

Add some ink: *My thoughts and prayers on this day;*

_____

_____

_____

_____

_____

DAY 26

The Breath

*Millions have come, hungry to hear from God. Hundreds
of thousands have responded to His call to salvation and a
commitment to holiness, and a fresh charge has issued throughout
the world for holiness and fresh intimacy with God.*
JOHN KILPATRICK (BROWNSVILLE REVIVAL)

There are two holy Scripture verses that we know so well when it comes to the topic of revival:

Unless the LORD builds the house, they labour in vain who build it...
PSALMS 127:1 NKJV

'Not by might nor by power, but by My Spirit,' says the LORD of hosts.
ZECHARIAH 4:6 NKJV

There is such a big—even ridiculous—difference between what our might can accomplish and what the Spirit of God can. We cannot even compare the two. In Ezekiel Chapter 37 God asks, "Can these bones live, Ezekiel?" The most obvious answer is; 'Of course not, since when do dry bones live? Since when does a valley of dry bones turn into a living breathing army?'

*Again, He said to me, "Prophesy to these bones, and say to them, 'O dry bones, hear the word of the Lord!' Thus says the Lord God to these bones: 'Surely I will cause **breath** to enter into you, and you shall live.'"*
EZEKIEL 37:4-5 NKJV

Oh, the breath of God! What a work it can do in reviving and creating power and might... in comparison to what we can do! It can be likened to the difference between rowing a boat or sailing it. Can you imagine trying to row a boat around the world? The strength, the energy, the effort, the endurance—impossible! You cannot row a boat around the world, but you can definitely sail one.

I'm sure you can see in your mind a picture of a ship with its sail hoisted high being thrust through the waters at top speed as it is propelled by a mighty wind. Can you imagine being a sailor on that ship standing on the deck, water spraying in your face looking up at the sails full of wind and in awe of the raw power thrusting you forward?

That's what I imagine it must feel like being in the middle of a revival! What could the Lord do with one local church that has raised its sail in the right direction? The answer is: anything! Anything is possible with the Spirit of God—He could reach the whole world!

That's right, the whole world from one local church. I know that it doesn't add up. It doesn't seem possible. How could we possibly reach the world from one church? When you consider what resources are typically available the task is just preposterous. But this is what happens when revival comes. The breath of God fills the sails and anything becomes possible.

In 1995, revival hit the Assemblies of God church in Brownsville, USA. Over the next six years, God drew an average of 5,500 people per night. Can you imagine, for six years? They estimate a total of between 2.5 million and 4.5 million people coming to one local church, and those people came from 150 different nations! God simply threw a party and invited the world. Can you imagine 2,5million people coming through your church's doors in the next six years?

With all those people coming they decided to open a training school of ministry which equipped thousands of students and pastors who were then sent to do missionary work in 122 nations. Starting with what you have, could you train thousands of people and send them to 122 different nations to advance the Gospel?

It's "crazy-impossible" in human might and power! But, by the breath of God, anything is possible!

In that period the Brownsville church raised $117 million which was given away to missions; funding the Gospel in other nations. Could you raise that much money in that period of time?

Let's read that scripture again and let it sink in:

Unless the LORD builds the house, they labour in vain who build it...
PSALM 127:1 NKJV

There were many other exciting things about the Brownsville revival; nearly 200,000 people gave their lives to Jesus and hundreds of thousands had their faith renewed. Marriages were restored, addictions were broken, sins were renounced and many were physically and emotionally healed.

There were a couple of things this church had before revival hit; namely two-and-a half-years (30 months) of intentional prayer for revival and a deep heart to win the world for Christ. They hoisted a sail of faith, they asked God to come and use their little boat and He did. He took them on a journey around the world that was unthinkable, unimaginable. So, let's hoist our sail of faith, let's aim our heart at nations and let's ask for the breath of God to fill it.

And so we pray...

Lord, I bow my heart and bend my knee,
send revival, and start with me;
Pour out your Spirit in an unprecedented way;
May all who hear be saved today;
May all who are saved proclaim the Way;
Lord send revival and start with me.

Add some ink: *My thoughts and prayers on this day;*

_____

_____

_____

_____

_____

DAY 27

Sowing with Tears and Reaping with Joy

Those who sow in tears shall reap in joy.
He who continually goes forth weeping,
Bearing seed for sowing, Shall doubtless come again with rejoicing,
Bringing his sheaves with him.
PSALM 126:5-6 NKJV

The law of sowing and reaping is not only written into the agricultural code of the earth but also into the spiritual laws that govern our lives and future. The principle is: There can be no harvest without sowing.

When a farmer plants seed, there is never a guarantee of what will happen, yet he MUST sow anyway. The only thing he is guaranteed is that if he does not sow he will not reap.

The same is true with revival. Revival is harvest time. However, harvest time does not come without a time of sowing. Revival comes because someone sowed the seeds of revival. To have a natural harvest—someone has to plough the ground, plant the seed, and then water it in expectation that God will make it grow.

Likewise with revival, someone has to labour in prayer and intercession preparing the ground and sowing seeds of faith. We also have to sow the Word of God and pray for the rain to fall in season in expectation that God will make the seeds germinate.

Jesus said the following to His disciples when crowds from the city of Sychar came pouring out to find Him:

W. Samuel Sandeman

*I sent you to **reap** that for which you have not laboured; others*
have laboured, and you have entered into their labours.
JOHN 4:38 NKJV

He was talking about the huge crowd of people approaching them hungry for the Gospel of the Kingdom of God. That crowd of people was the harvest, and the disciples were the fortunate ones who would reap. However, Jesus acknowledged that the moment would not have happened if others had not laboured and sown. That huge crowd and revival that took place was not an accident. Somebody did something to make that moment possible.

John the Baptist had to come before Jesus to prepare the way. His role was to reignite the conscience of the nation and bring them back to a place of devout worship free of the hypocrisy of religion... so that Jesus could come and reap. When the crowds turned from following John to Jesus, he said: *"He must increase but I must decrease..."* (John 3:30 NKJV) In other words my job is done.

How many others were preparing the way for Jesus' revival ministry we are not sure, but I believe there were many. I think of Simeon and Anna both devout people of prayer and fasting who were looking for the promise of God expectantly, living in anticipation of prophetic words, praying those prophetic words into being and sowing something into the atmosphere of Jerusalem that would prepare the climate for Jesus' revival ministry.

I'm sure we would all prefer to be in the harvest team, but someone has to sow. Both processes are laborious, but one is a labour of joy the other is a labour of faith, hope and endurance.

We all enjoy walking down an avenue of beautiful trees in full bloom, but years before we experience the beauty of such a moment somebody had a street with no trees. Nothing growing. All they had was a shovel and some seed and a hope of what could be. A long-term picture and expectation that they might see what they hoped.

So it is with those who pray for revival. They are the sowers. They are the ones who carry a picture of what could be and they plant seeds of faith into the atmosphere of their schools, campuses, churches, and cities, in expectation that God will cause those seeds to germinate into miracles of conviction, repentance, salvation, healing, and deliverance.

They are typically the unsung heroes of revivals; they are not named. They are not on the stage. But we know they are vital! They were there with tears when no one was looking. They started the prayer meetings, they got up early when others slept in. They went to bed late, if at all. They sacrificed meals and they ploughed into the spiritual ground with groanings too deep for words. They laboured. Would there have been a restoration of Israel if men like Daniel and Nehemiah had not sown for it with prayers, fasting, and tears?

How many people I know who are in the kingdom today because their mom, husband, wife, or friend engaged the spiritual law of sowing in prayer for their lost soul. Maybe you are in the kingdom and serving the Lord because of such prayers. I know that I am. There can be no harvest without sowing.

There is one fundamental difference between sowing in the natural and sowing in the spiritual. When farmers sow seed, they are never sure of what will happen to their seed. We on the other hand are totally sure:

> *Those who sow in tears* **Shall** *reap in joy. He who continually goes forth weeping, Bearing seed for sowing,* **Shall doubtless** *come again with rejoicing, Bringing his sheaves with him.*
> PSALMS 126:5-6 NKJV (emphasis added)

W. Samuel Sandeman

So let us continue to sow and charge the atmosphere with faith for what we believe God will do.

And so we pray...

Lord, I bow my heart and bend my knee,
send revival, and start with me;
Pour out your Spirit in an unprecedented way;
May all who hear be saved today;
May all who are saved proclaim the Way;
Lord send revival and start with me.

Add some ink: *My thoughts and prayers on this day;*

_____

_____

_____

_____

_____

DAY 28

Draw Near

Oh, that You would rend the heavens! That You would come down! That the mountains might shake at Your presence...
ISAIAH 64:1 NKJV

We have said that revival is God coming near, and what a beautiful thing that is! Oh, how we want Him to draw near and descend! This is the heart cry of a revivalist.

We want God to come down in all His magnificence and we want those mountains to shake with His presence. Everything and everyone, proud and obstinate, to shake. Everything resistant and in the way of the kingdom to shake. We want Him to shake our schools, neighbourhoods, and churches…

This is our cry!

However, if revival is God drawing near, then praying for revival must be us drawing near to God.

The principle is found in the book of James where it says: *"Draw near to God and He will draw near to you…"* (James 4:8 NKJV).

If God is to draw near to us, we must first draw near to Him. The onus is on us to take the first step. 'Draw near to God'—now that's a thought worth exploring! I think of Moses who drew near to the burning bush, only once he had drawn near did God speak. God was actually waiting to see if he would draw near (Exodus 3:3-4). Thereafter, Moses kept drawing near to God all his life.

W. Samuel Sandeman

When the cloud descended on Mount Sinai, there was thunder, lightning, fire, smoke, and a loud trumpet blast, that made everyone drawback in terror. It says in Exodus;

*So the people stood afar off, but Moses **drew near**
the thick darkness where God was.*
EXODUS 20:21 NKJV

Moses kept drawing near to God and God kept drawing near to Moses. If we are praying for God to come near, we must first be willing to draw near to Him. We cannot simply ask God to come down without there first being an ascending of our lives to God.

But what does that mean? What does it mean that we must ascend, and draw near?

Well, typically we think drawing near means we start praying. This is true. When we pray we are drawing near to God. However, there is more to this principle of drawing near... so much more!

Drawing near to God is not just saying prayers, it is bringing our whole life to Him. We have this staggering ability to detach our prayers from our lives. You know what I mean, we say all the right things—the things we should say in prayer—but then we go and live a life that is not close to God, maybe even distant.

Drawing near to God is about bringing our whole lives to Him. He has already said He does not want people to draw near with their lips, yet their hearts are far from Him (Matthew 15:8). Our prayers cannot be one thing, and our lives something else.

We cannot stand afar and send words to God. God is not interested in just words arriving in His sanctuary, He wants to know what hearts are attached to those words and who said those words. Words never move God, it's pure hearts that move Him. It's people whose lives match the sincerity of their prayers that see God move:

For the eyes of the Lord run to and fro throughout
the whole earth to show Himself strong in behalf of
those whose hearts are blameless toward Him.
2 CHRONICLES 16:9 AMPC

If we want God to show Himself strong as He does in revival, let us be a people who are practicing the art of a blameless heart.

Who may ascend into the hill of the LORD? Or who may stand
in His holy place? He who has clean hands and a pure heart...
PSALM 24:3-5 NKJV

Who may ascend? Who may draw near? People who are willing to consecrate themselves. People who live holy lives, who live righteously. Didn't Jesus say, *"Blessed are the pure in heart, for they shall see God"*? Drawing near to God is not just praying, it is about committing to a life of holiness. One where we take every thought captive into the obedience of Christ. We guard our mouths, relationships, and hearts. We confess our wrong motives. We do the daily grind of denying our flesh so that the life of Christ might shine brighter in us. It means becoming more godly, more godlike in our conduct, forgiving, releasing, blessing, loving. This is what it means to draw near to Him... we bring Him our lives.

Behind every revival, we find people who didn't just pray the right things, say the right things, but people who committed to drawing near to God. So, the journey to revival is not just a commitment to prayer it is a commitment to holiness. Have you made that commitment?

Many times in scripture the call went out for the people of God to consecrate themselves. Why? Because God was about to come down and do great and mighty things in their midst (Joshua

3:5). God needed His people to be prepared for His presence. Consecration comes before conquest. A commitment to holiness comes before revival.

So, as we pray this morning for revival—which is God coming near—let us remember that He doesn't just want our words but our lives. Let us be the people who not only make prayer our daily priority and delight but holiness as well!

And so we pray...

Lord, I bow my heart and bend my knee,
send revival, and start with me;
Pour out your Spirit in an unprecedented way;
May all who hear be saved today;
May all who are saved proclaim the Way;
Lord send revival and start with me.

Add some ink: *My thoughts and prayers on this day;*

_____

_____

_____

_____

_____

DAY 29

The Power of Holiness

Behold, the LORD's hand is not shortened, That it cannot save...
ISAIAH 59:1 NKJV

The reason that we need revival is and has always been because of one thing: our sin.

The pattern is the same: God's people become compromised and worldly, more in tune with the flesh and less in love with the things of God and the mission of God. Self-glory becomes their obsession and not His glory in the nations. We become more consumed by our temporal lives than eternal matters and less like Christ in the way we live. Scientists have a term, "entropy" which describes the natural inclination of the things of this world to move from a state of order to a state of chaos, if there is no outside intervention. Things move from a state of perfection to imperfection. This includes humans, which includes Christians. John Wimber used to say that we get filled with the Holy Spirit, but we leak. When this happens, we lose the beautiful fellowship and communion we should have with God. Equally as tragic we lose the anointing of God's Spirit, which can be termed "the burden-destroying power of God" that is meant to characterise the church and propel her in the mission of God.

W. Samuel Sandeman

Adulterers and adulteresses! Do you not know that friendship with the world is enmity with God? Whoever therefore wants to be a friend of the world makes himself an enemy of God. Or do you think that the Scripture says in vain, 'The Spirit who dwells in us yearns jealously'?
JAMES 4:4-5 NKJV

God's spirit yearns for His bride, but cannot and will not cohabit with her and the world. So, when the church chooses the World and lays in the arms of sin as Samson lay in the arms of Delilah, the friendship of God's presence lifts and the anointing leaves in the same way that Samson had his power stripped away when Delilah cut his hair. Church then becomes routine and carnal, driven in human strength, religious in many ways, and mostly unfruitful, save a devout few. Shepherds grow weary and frustrated with their sheep. Nominal becomes normal. As the church becomes more nominal, society becomes more corrupt because as the church goes, so goes society. Without salt and light, without "a city set on a hill", darkness and decay set in.

What is most tragic in this commonly repeated pattern is how long it can take before the people of God know from where they have fallen. As the presence and anointing lift, many don't even notice. Sometimes it can be generations before somebody rises and says, *"This is not how it should be; we are not as we should be, change is needed! God is needed! The church must come alive"*

This awareness is the first sign change is near. It is the grace of God in operation. The Spirit searches for a few and begins to whisper an alternate future and to stir a desire for something more. This is a stirring of the Spirit. We see an example of the stirring of the Holy Spirit in Haggai:

So, the LORD stirred up the spirit of Zerubbabel the son of Shealtiel,
governor of Judah, and the spirit of Joshua the son of Jehozadak, the
high priest, and the spirit of all the remnant of the people; and they
came and worked on the house of the LORD of hosts, their God...
HAGGAI 1:14 NKJV

What follows the stirring is a returning to the work of the Lord, a drawing near to Him in prayer and as that happens holiness becomes a top priority of those who long for revival. Holiness becomes an innate necessity in our pursuit, a declaration of our desperation, evidence of our return, and undeniable proof of our wholeheartedness in what we seek:

Pursue peace with all people, and holiness,
without which no one will see the Lord.
HEBREWS 12:14 NKJV

If it was sin that led to the church's demise, it can be nothing less than holiness that sees the church return to its glory. What we see in revival history is that each revival is preceded by a deep longing and return to holiness for those seeking revival. For us right now this must be our posture and purpose for It is the... *earnest and heartfelt prayer of a* **righteous** *man that makes tremendous power available.* (James 5:16)

Now, as we pray for revival, let us pray for our hearts to return fully to the state of holiness, that revival really would start with us, that we might become more conscious of holiness and aware of what brings His pleasure and the friendship and fellowship of the Spirit.

And so we pray...

Lord, I bow my heart and bend my knee,
send revival, and start with me;
Pour out your Spirit in an unprecedented way;
May all who hear be saved today;
May all who are saved proclaim the Way;
Lord send revival and start with me.

Add some ink: *My thoughts and prayers on this day;*

_____

_____

_____

_____

_____

DAY 30

Music

Just prior to the revival, the McGregors, South African brothers ministering in powerfully anointed music ministry, visited Brownsville to conduct a series of revival services. The heightened presence of the Holy Spirit during those services led many to wonder what might be happening in the spiritual realm, and when revival shortly broke out, the consensus was that these services had done much to prepare the spiritual atmosphere for God's mighty visitation.

BROWNSVILLE CHURCH

Music captures and expresses moments in ways that speaking cannot. heaven is full of music and in revival the veil between heaven and earth becomes thin. In recent prayer meetings in Durban, people have heard worship music that was not being played in the natural; a sign that heaven is opening up and revival is on its way. The sounds of heaven are heard and the songs of heaven are released. As some have said, '*it is worth having revival just for the music…*'

In revival, some songs are written and sung that capture the climate of heaven and express the heart of God at the moment. Sometimes they are old songs, that just come alive in a new way. Sometimes they are new songs written out of the experience of what God is saying and doing in that moment.

In the Welsh revival of 1904, there was a special anointing on the old hymn "Here is Love" written by the Welshman, William

Rees. Singing in those days was often spontaneous. People arrived at church to sing. They didn't have professional worship teams performing for them. The song "Here is Love" would be one song that had a special anointing on it. It became known as the love song of the Welsh revival and was used mightily by God during that time. As the anointing can flow through ministers of the Gospel, the anointing can also flow through a song. As revivalists would preach from the pulpits the spirit would work in the pews leading people to repentance and faith as well as healing and deliverance. Songs would do the same. Just by singing "Here is Love" God's presence would descend, while heartfelt repentance and a filling of the Spirit would follow. The words to "Here is Love" are:

Here is love, vast as the ocean,
Lovingkindness as the flood,
When the Prince of life, our Ransom,
Shed for us His precious blood.
Who His love will not remember?
Who can cease to sing His praise?
He can never be forgotten
Throughout Heav'n's eternal days.
On the mount of crucifixion,
Fountains opened deep and wide;
Through the floodgates of God's mercy
Flowed a vast and gracious tide.
Grace and love, like mighty rivers,
Poured incessant from above.
And Heav'n's peace and perfect justice
Kissed a guilty world in love.

You can quickly see why this song carried such an anointing at that time. The words so aptly capture what revival is:

> *Through the floodgates of God's mercy*
> *Flowed a vast and gracious tide*
> *Grace and love like mighty rivers*
> *Poured incessant from above*

Is there any better description of what a revival is?

> *Heaven's peace and perfect justice, Kissed a guilty world in love'*

Revival is *a kiss from heaven on a guilty world.* It is *God's floodgates of mercy pouring out incessantly from above.*

In Azusa Street, many songs were sung and written under the anointing of the moment. However, the best were the songs of the spirit. A first-hand witness of the revival, evangelist Frank Bartleman, wrote this account of what was at the time an entirely new phenomenon—they had no reference point for it or theology to understand it:

> *It was exercised as the Spirit moved the possessors, either in solo fashion or by the company. It was sometimes without words, other times in tongues. The effect was wonderful on the people. It brought a heavenly atmosphere as though the angels themselves were present and joining with us. And possibly they were. In fact, it was the very breath of God, playing on human heartstrings, or human vocal cords. The notes were wonderful in sweetness, volume, and duration. In fact, they were of times humanly impossible. It was 'singing in the Spirit.'*

I find it without coincidence that many songs and albums have come out recently singing for revival— they are prayer songs from around the world, and I believe they are the stirring of the Spirit.

Open up the heavens, pour out your presence, we want to see revival,
Bring us back to you, oh how we need you to, we want to see revival."
Only you make darkness shake only you
Only you make dry bones awake
REVIVAL BY JESUS CULTURE

Another recent song says:

Lord send revival, Lord send it now, a move
of your Spirit, heaven break out.
Come now in power, cover this land
Like you have done it before, would you do it again
LORD SEND REVIVAL BY HILLSONG YOUNG AND FREE

And then there is also:

Come awaken your people
Come awaken your city
Oh God of revival, pour it out, pour it out.
GOD OF REVIVAL BY BETHEL MUSIC

Today, let's join in with the global anthem for revival. God is certainly stirring many hearts for the same thing. Lift your voice and let a song of the Spirit flow heavenward for our God is on the move.

And so we pray...

Lord, I bow my heart and bend my knee,
send revival, and start with me;
Pour out your Spirit in an unprecedented way;
May all who hear be saved today;
May all who are saved proclaim the Way;
Lord send revival and start with me.

Add some ink: *My thoughts and prayers on this day;*

_____

_____

_____

_____

_____

DAY 31

Power

... stay here in the city until you are clothed
with the mighty power of heaven.
LUKE 24:49 TPT

The words 'church' and 'power' should be synonymous. Jesus instructed His disciples to wait until they were 'clothed with the mighty power of heaven.'

In other words: '*Guys, when you go out into the world, I want you to be clothed in power, don't go anywhere until that happens*'. Jesus wants His Church to be clothed in power. Wearing power like a new jacket. He wants us to be attached to it and it to us. Where we go, it goes. Like Joseph's coat of many colours, it should define us and by it, we should be known.

Paul knew this and he was determined that his ministry would never slip into just wise persuasive words. He didn't want people's faith to rest in his wisdom or anybody else's. He wanted their faith to rest in the living and powerful God. He wanted people to know that the God they believed in is a powerful God. He wrote to the church in the city of Corinth:

And my speech and my preaching were not with persuasive words of
human wisdom, but in demonstration of the Spirit and of power, that
your faith should not be in the wisdom of men but in the power of God.
I CORINTHIANS 2:4-5 NKJV

When John the Baptist had a moment of doubt, He sent word to Jesus saying; *'Are You the Coming One, or do we look for another?'* (Luke 7:20 NKJV) Jesus replied:

> *Go and tell John the things you have seen and heard: that the blind see, the lame walk, the lepers are cleansed, the deaf hear, the dead are raised, the poor have the Gospel preached to them. And blessed is he who is not offended because of Me."*
> LUKE 7:22-23 NKJV

In saying this, Jesus affirmed that the power of God is what authenticated His ministry. He said to another crowd of people that were full of doubts… *"If I do not do the miraculous works of My Father, do not believe Me; but if I do, though you do not believe Me, believe the works, that you may know and believe that the Father is in Me, and I in Him"* (John 10:37-38 NKJV).

The miraculous works were signs pointing to His identity… evidence that proved who He was. The miraculous works supported His claim to be the Son of God and the Messiah. When the early disciples were threatened not to preach the message of Jesus, they prayed as follows:

> *'So now, Lord, listen to their threats to harm us. **Empower** us, as your servants, to speak the word of God freely and courageously. Stretch out **your hand of power** through us to heal, and to move in signs and wonders by the name of your holy Son, Jesus!' At that moment the earth shook beneath them, causing the building they were in to tremble. Each one of them was filled with the Holy Spirit, and they proclaimed the word of God with unrestrained boldness.*
> ACTS 4:29-31 TPT

Note what they asked for: They asked for power from God. Why? The power of God is what proves the message. Power to heal is what demonstrates the love of God. God never intended His Church to be just words and no evidence. God's combination is word and works; message and manifestation.

They prayed: *"Stretch out your hand of power **through us** to heal and to move in signs and wonders..."* If they prayed for this, I think we can too. God answered their prayer, as evidence that this is His will.

Notice that God stretches His hand of power *through us*. We are His hands through which His hand of power moves. Think about that! It's like they were praying; *'put us on like a glove and show the world who Jesus is.'*

When power is missing and all we have to offer lost and sick people is wise words and eloquent thoughts... then revival is what is needed. Revival is pulling out the jump leads connecting them to the dead battery of a vehicle and giving it a supercharge so the engine can roar again and move forward in power. When we pray, *'send revival and start with me'* we are saying; *'we need a jump start, Lord, our defining attribute is missing!'*

In the Cane Ridge revival of 1801, a huge crowd came away for a weekend of spiritual renewal. So big was the crowd that there were several preachers set up in different parts of the grounds who would all preach at the same time with the same goal in mind. People would gather around different preachers and listen, here is James Finley's account of the moment:

The noise was like the roar of Niagara. The vast sea of human beings seemed to be agitated as if by a storm. I counted seven ministers, all preaching at one time, some on stumps, others in wagons, and one standing on a tree which had, in falling, lodged against another. I stepped up on a log where I could have a better view of the surging sea of humanity. The scene that then presented itself to my mind was indescribable. At one time I saw at least five hundred people swept down by the power of God in a moment as if a battery of a thousand guns had been opened upon them, and then immediately followed shrieks and shouts that rent the very heavens.

What happened? God's power came as the Gospel was proclaimed. It came and it authenticated the message. It followed the message like the tails of a coat follow its owner. It knocked hundreds of people off their feet. And it knocked the devil out of them— literally, as demons left with screams. The story of James Finley is that he arrived as a curious backslidden Christian, but after such a power encounter he went on to become a Methodist minister of great impact.

Another witness to the revival said:

The scene was awful beyond description; the falling, crying out, praying, exhorting, singing, shouting, - such new and striking evidences of a supernatural power, that few, if any could escape without being affected. Those who tried to run from the power and presence of God were frequently struck on the way, or impelled by some alarming signal to return and so powerful was the evidence on all sides, that no place was found for the obstinate sinner to shelter himself...

This is what happens when God comes near. When we pray for revival, we are asking for God to return to His bride the clothing that has been lost, stolen, or neglected. We are repenting for being content with human eloquence (or good coffee) and we are making space for God's power to come and be manifest amongst us. We are asking to be empowered from on high so that we can do the works of Jesus. Why? So that all would know there is a powerful God who loves them.

And so we pray...

Lord, I bow my heart and bend my knee,
send revival, and start with me;
Pour out your Spirit in an unprecedented way;
May all who hear be saved today;
May all who are saved proclaim the Way;
Lord send revival and start with me.

Add some ink: *My thoughts and prayers on this day;*

_____
_____
_____
_____
_____

DAY 32

God First and Foremost

*...For from him and through him and for him are
all things. To him be the glory forever! Amen.*
ROMANS 11:36

In the late 1700s, two beliefs were gaining popularity in
America, especially in the frontier states. They were the beliefs
of Universalism and Deism. Universalism is the belief that all
will be saved. Deism is the belief that God made the world but is
uninvolved in the world.

These two heretical beliefs are still very much alive today, I am
sure you might know a few people who think this way. They say, '*I'm
sure God will let me into heaven if heaven is real. There can't possibly be a
hell—a loving God would never do that.*' That is a modern expression
of universalism. Also, I'm sure you will know people who would say
that if there is a God, he definitely isn't around, or important, or
worth knowing. That is Deism.

These beliefs are like the anthem of our generation. They were
captured so precisely in the song *Imagine* by John Lennon of The
Beatles:

Imagine there's no heaven
It's easy if you try
No hell below us
Above us only sky
Imagine all the people living for today

Wherever these beliefs are deeply rooted you find moral decay. The reason is that they exclude final accountability and judgment. They exclude heaven and hell and worst of all they exclude God from everyday life. The fruit of believing that God will not judge us or that He is not around anyway is that we become a law unto ourselves and we live for today.

In the frontier states, these thoughts had grown into the fabric of society like weeds—they were everywhere and they were choking faith, morality, and righteousness.

Ministers in those days were struggling and reported: *"A prevalence of vice and infidelity, profanity, mistreatment of slaves, sexual immorality, rampant alcoholism, and avaricious land-grabbing, coupled with declining church membership."*

(Sounds much like our times!) In 1798 the Presbyterian General Assembly asked that a day be set aside for fasting, humiliation, and prayer to redeem the frontier from what they called an "*Egyptian darkness*".

To say the church was on the back foot was an understatement. They had been relegated to the side-lines and were almost obscure. However, after much prayer and repentance, there was a general sense of hope that God was about to move in a new way. No one was sure when or where it would begin, but many were convinced that God would begin His work of revival.

The first spark came in a Presbyterian church. It was a weekend conference with nothing unusual or worth reporting until right at the end of the last sermon, God touched one woman. Soon the whole congregation sat weeping, and then the power of the Holy Spirit came. Preacher John McGee began preaching under the power of the Holy Spirit and soon the floor was covered with people slain in the Spirit.

That spark led to many more meetings and weekend events which culminated in the Cane Ridge revival where John McGee said: *"Many thousands of people attended. The mighty power and mercy of God was manifested. The people fell before the Word, like corn before a storm of wind, and many rose from the dust with divine glory shining in their countenances."*

When the Spirit fell in the upper room on the Day of Pentecost, back in Israel, some prophesied, some spoke in tongues, Peter preached and the crowds were cut to the heart in repentance. The same happened at these revival meetings in Cane Ridge: some began to prophesy, some spoke in tongues, some fell under the power, some were cut to the heart and some started to preach. One story worth mentioning is that of a 7-year-old girl who mounted a man's shoulders and preached wondrous words until she fell asleep. There were many accounts of children preaching and declaring visions and amazing God encounters.

What was clear about those years of revival was the power of God. After those meetings, there was no doubt left in anyone's mind that God was very much involved in human life and the reality of heaven, hell, and judgment will be faced by all. Some mockers came to these revivals and even tried to oppose and jeer the preachers, however many of them were even struck under the power of God the moment they opened their mouths!

The result of those few years of revival was the complete transformation of the whole frontier: one man traveling through the frontier reported that he heard *"little else than the great revival* of *religion.*" In other words, God was once again first a foremost in society... His revival had done its work!

When society becomes lost in beliefs like Deism, Universalism, Humanism, Marxism or Agnosticism, what is needed is revival. Can you imagine God becoming first and foremost in our society again? Is there not a need? Then let's pray for revival!

And so we pray...

Lord, I bow my heart and bend my knee,
send revival, and start with me;
Pour out your Spirit in an unprecedented way;
May all who hear be saved today;
May all who are saved proclaim the Way;
Lord send revival and start with me.

Add some ink: *My thoughts and prayers on this day;*

_____

_____

_____

_____

_____

DAY 33

Friendship with God

There is more than enough room in my Father's home. If this were not so, would I have told you that I am going to prepare a place for you? When everything is ready, I will come and get you, so that you will always be with me where I am.
JOHN 14:2-3 NLT

These are some of the last words Jesus said to His disciples. I don't think we really comprehend how much God loves us and wants to be with us. Sometimes it is just 'theology' to us; mere words. But if we look at the Word of God, we see a God who wants us, who likes us, who has a home with more than enough room for all of us. Jesus has gone to prepare a place for us and then will come back and get us. It even sounds like He is quite excited to show us this new place He has made for us!

We live in the period of history when Jesus is "away." Is that a problem for us? Well, Jesus promised that while He is away, *'I am <u>not</u> going to leave you orphans...'* (John 14:18 NKJV).

Before that promise, He made another promise, saying; *"I will ask the Father and He will give you another Saviour, the Holy Spirit of Truth, who will be to you a friend just like me—and He will never leave you..."* (John 14:16-17 TPT)

God does not want us to be alone. He wants to be with us. Better still, He doesn't just want to be around us but in us. Jesus said; *"My Father and I will come and make our home <u>in</u> [you]"*; you don't get closer than that—this is the most intimate connection possible.

We have said that revival is God coming near and we have spoken of how many wonderful things happen when God does come near. We could talk forever of those wonderful things. There are also many wonderful after-effects of revival: we have spoken of missions, and transformation of society, but until now there is one after-effect we have not mentioned. This after-effect or fruit of revival is probably one of the sweetest blessings of revival and definitely one of the reasons He would send revival; and that is the restoration of personal intimate connection with God.

Revival comes in waves of power and signs and wonders in church meetings and outside. Then, after the meetings, we all go home and enjoy a sweet and intimate renewed connection and fellowship with God. The one we were designed for, the one that Adam had in the garden... walking and talking with God in the cool of the day. Have you ever wondered what on earth God and Adam spoke about? There was no crime, corruption or sin requiring Adam to intercede for. No, there was no pandemic requiring desperate prayers of protection. Adam had no needs to ask for (except maybe a wife), or debts needing to be paid; no illness and no sick relatives; no healings required. There was nothing wrong with the world. They had nothing but friendship; two beings enjoying each other's company.

We so often relate to God out of crisis, desperation, and needs—our needs or the needs of a broken world, but have you thought about what might exist between us and God without any crisis? Do we still need Him, want Him? If everything is as it should be and we are well and healthy, do we still seek His company for nothing but enjoying His company? He does. And we should too, because

W. Samuel Sandeman

the Word tells us that in His presence there is joy and at His right hand, pleasures forever more.

It wasn't just with Adam; Abraham is called a friend of God three times in Scripture. Moses was called that as well. In John chapter 15 Jesus upgraded His disciples from 'servants' to being 'friends'. God certainly doesn't have to use this language with us—I mean He is God—we can just stay servants. But He does use this language. He wants friendship. He wants to be a part of our lives and live in intimate connection with each of us. This is one of God's pleasures.

Jesus said: *"If anyone loves Me, he will keep My word; and My Father will love him, and We will come to him and make Our home with him."*
JOHN 14:23 NKJV

We will come and do what? Make our home with them!? We can be a home to God, not just a house. Is that not the most amazing promise: God the Father and God the Son living in us! The best life on earth is not having fame or fortune but being a home for the Lord and having His loving, peaceful, joyful presence. Nothing else is better. No promised land is worth having without His presence, friendship with God is ultimate.

When this fellowship is lost what is needed is revival, for the after-effect of revival is a return to doing life <u>with</u> God. Talking, laughing, listening, asking, and all while we do the most mundane tasks of cooking, driving, typing, cleaning, or running.

Revival is the breaking of ground, the hardness of heart, the washing of repentance, the healing of the soul, the deliverance from darkness, the breaking of addictions, the throwing away of idols. It is the dramatic and needed resuscitation to bring us back to life… but what kind of life? What life would He want us to come back to? Clearly, a life lived with Him. This is what we were designed for and where we are most satisfied and even where we are the most effective and brilliant.

And He who sent Me is with Me. The Father has not left Me alone, for I always do those things that please Him.
JOHN 8:29 NKJV

Jesus lived with His Father. He was never alone. This is how we should do life… Unbroken fellowship with the Father through the Holy Spirit, because we do those things that please Him. It is worth having a revival just to get us back to that place of intimate daily friendship with God. So, as we pray for revival let's pray for a restoration of our friendship with God and that those who have never tasted such would be awakened to the best life possible—being a friend of God.

And so we pray...

Lord, I bow my heart and bend my knee,
send revival, and start with me;
Pour out your Spirit in an unprecedented way;
May all who hear be saved today;
May all who are saved proclaim the Way;
Lord send revival and start with me.

Add some ink: *My thoughts and prayers on this day;*

_____

_____

_____

_____

_____

DAY 34

Times of Refreshing

Believe in me so that rivers of living water will burst out from within you, flowing from your innermost being, just like the Scripture says!
JOHN 7:38 TPT

In John Chapter 7 Jesus spoke about the Holy Spirit that would come and live within us, that He, the Holy Spirit would be like a river bursting out from within us. Rivers are beautiful because they are a source of life and power. To have a river bursting from our innermost being is to have a source of life, power, and beauty flowing from us to the world. That is the Christian life; the life Jesus wants us to have!

I am not sure which particular Scripture Jesus was referring to when He spoke those words *"just like the Scripture says"* for there are many prophecies in the Old Testament that speak of God making rivers in the wilderness. One is found in Psalms 78: *"He split open the rocks in the wilderness to give them water, as from a gushing spring. He made streams pour from the rock, making the waters flow down like a river!"* (Psalm 78:15-16 NLT).

God brought water from rocks! If ever there was a picture of salvation that would be it! We were like rocks in the wilderness, hardened by sin, living in a dry and hostile territory, a world without God. Then through repentance and the Gospel being preached to us, we are split open miraculously and when we receive the gift of the Holy Spirit a new life source bursts from within us... a river of life flows from us to a thirsty people. There could not be a better picture of salvation and the resultant fruitful life that comes from living in the power of the Holy Spirit.

That is the powerful, miracle-working, transformative nature of our God. He makes water come out of dry places (people!) we never thought water could come from.

R. Edward Miller and his wife discovered this as missionaries to Argentina. They were sown into hard ground. No one was interested in their ministry. They tried hard, but the climate in Argentina was so spiritually dry. There was no passion for God or even any interest.

Before giving up and leaving the country they set themselves to pray. And pray they did for hours every day and for months. Then, one day, God's presence broke through their arid climate and Edward experienced his own powerful personal encounter with God. Revival started with him. God then told Edward that revival would come to Argentina. He told Him to start a prayer meeting and pray each evening. In obedience, Edward put the invitation out and only three people attended—that's how dry it was! But God never needs a majority or a massive army to work with; three people are enough.

After only four nights of prayer one woman in the meeting had felt led to bang on the table with her hand, and when she did, They were all filled with the radiant power of the Holy Spirit and began speaking in tongues. Revival had come! The Holy Spirit had burst forth and rushing water spread rapidly! The church filled up, people came from all over, and were supernaturally touched by the refreshing power of God.

When Peter preached to the crowd at Pentecost revival, he said: *"repent and turn back to God so that your sins will be removed, and so that times of **refreshing** will stream from the Lord's presence."* (Acts 3:19 TPT)

Revival is '*times of refreshing*' streaming from the Lord's presence! This is what Edward Miller and his wife experienced. They had dug a well, they had struck water and it was gushing out. As people came, they were filled. In turn, they would go out like a stream of witnesses flowing in the supernatural life-giving power of God all over Argentina.

In this Argentinian revival there was an account of two young people who were touched by God and went to visit a woman whose mother was paralysed and had been in bed for five years. They prayed for her, and she was miraculously healed! Another account tells of two elderly people who visited a man who had been in a coma. He was crippled and his liver had been damaged from excessive drinking. They prayed for him and he was instantly healed! Doesn't that sound like a river of life flowing out of the church? Rocks had been split open and were now gushing with life-giving power.

I imagine Edward Miller and his wife as farmers, in a dry, dusty land, picking up their spades day by day and digging for water not knowing when or if they would find any. But then one day water trickles from the ground and their hopes are answered; yes, there is water here! When they started that prayer meeting, it was like three others picked up spades and joined in and when that woman banged her hand down on the table it was like striking a divine artery. They were now all refreshed and had a fountain that could touch a nation. All the prayer was suddenly worth it!

For I am about to do something new. See, I have already begun!
Do you not see it? I will make a pathway through the wilderness.
I will create rivers in the dry wasteland... Yes, I will make rivers
in the dry wasteland so my chosen people can be refreshed.
Isaiah 43:19-20 NLT

W. Samuel Sandeman

It doesn't matter how spiritually dry the climate is. Even if it feels like we are living in a wilderness and people don't care about God. We must know that God can split open rocks and cause them to gush with water.

I love that story of Edward and his wife; so faithful to persist against such great odds! I love the fact that the moment that changed everything was when that woman banged her hand on the table. Why did she feel she needed to bang her hand on the table? I don't know, but she was clearly led by the Holy Spirit. The picture that I have in my mind is of someone who has had enough and puts down a demand with raw emotion; saying '*I will not settle for anything less!*' There is something about heartfelt prayer that moves God... I hope we are getting to that place. Let us put our spades in the soil again today and let's pray for rivers to burst forth in all the dry places around us, starting with our own hearts.

And so we pray...

> *Lord, I bow my heart and bend my knee,*
> *send revival, and start with me;*
> *Pour out your Spirit in an unprecedented way;*
> *May all who hear be saved today;*
> *May all who are saved proclaim the Way;*
> *Lord send revival and start with me.*

Add some ink: *My thoughts and prayers on this day;*

_____

_____

_____

_____

W. Samuel Sandeman

DAY 35

Pentecost

*He has anointed me to proclaim **the acceptable year** of the Lord.*
LUKE 4:18-19 NLT

The word Pentecost means *'fifty'* in Greek. It was fifty days from the Passover celebration where the children of Israel left Egypt in such a dramatic finale of placing blood on their doorposts, until they arrived at Mount Sinai where Moses received the Ten Commandments and the Law.

The Ten Commandments have been hailed as the foundation of the Western and free world. The giving of the Law at Mount Sinai was a powerful and significant moment for the world. The Law of God reveals God's righteous standard. It exposes sin. It tells us how to live. The apostle Paul said, *"...I would not have known sin except through the law. For I would not have known covetousness unless the law had said, 'You shall not covet'"* (Romans 7:7 NKJV).

Jesus ratified, validated, and upheld the law that was given to Moses. He said the greatest commandment is the first one: *"Love the Lord with all your heart mind and strength"* (Matthew 22:37). He said that adultery is not just the act with another person, but even to look with lust at another person constituted adultery in the heart. He said murder is not just the act, but if you hate your brother in your heart without cause, you are as guilty as a murderer (Matthew 5).

Jesus taught that even in the unseen world of our heart and thoughts we are to obey the law of God. The law that was given at Mount Sinai shows us God's righteous standard on how we are to relate to God and people. The Law was a gift from God to humanity. We would be lost without the Law of God.

The fact that it was 50 days from Passover to the giving of the law is also significant. Fifty is a significant number in the Bible. It is five tens. Five is the number of grace and ten is the number of completeness; most of us have ten fingers and ten toes. There were ten plagues of judgment on Egypt and there were Ten Commandments given.

Mathematically, 5×10 = grace x completeness = complete grace. God's revelation of the law at Mount Sinai was complete grace extended to humanity. However, as perfect, revealing and directing as God's law is, it has no power to help us sinners. The Law just shows us all what sinners we really are. It leaves us all defenceless and condemned. There is no one who has managed to keep it. That is, there was no one until Jesus.

Jesus was the only one who was without sin; the only one who followed the law perfectly. At Passover, we remember that He was the perfect sacrifice to cover our sins. But what would God give to us 50 days after such a perfect sacrifice, the very day Israel celebrated the giving of the law? He gave us another gift of complete grace. The gift of the Holy Spirit.

Where the law left us powerless, condemned, separated from God; the Holy Spirit empowers us to live a righteous life and seals our salvation, our sonship and acceptance back to God.

Now, the number 50 is also significant because it is the number that comes after 49 (you probably know that already!) You probably also know that the square root of 49 is 7. In other words, 49 is seven sevens ($7 \times 7 = 49$). God set in motion a system of work six days and rest on the seventh day. He also set in motion a calendar of work six years and rest on the seventh year. After seven cycles of working six years and resting on the seventh, you get to the 49th year at which point He instructed another 'bonus year' of rest being the fiftieth year. It was called the year of Jubilee. It was a year where Israel was instructed to forgive all debts, let all slaves go free, and return land to its original owners. It was instituted to break the cycle of debt and slavery. Hallelujah!

Did Jesus have anything to say about the Year of Jubilee? Yes, Jesus began His ministry with a clear reference to the year of Jubilee. In the synagogue at Nazareth, He read these words from Isaiah:

> *The Spirit of the Lord is upon Me, Because He has anointed Me To preach the Gospel to the poor; He has sent Me to heal the broken-hearted, to proclaim liberty to the captives and recovery of sight to the blind, to set at liberty those who are oppressed; to proclaim the acceptable year of the Lord.*
> LUKE 4:18-19 NKJV

The 'acceptable year' is the Jubilee year. His ministry marked the fulfilment of the Jubilee year. He set captives free. He partnered with the Father to release us from our eternal debt to God for our sins. He did this by paying our debts with his life. Then, 50 days after paying our debts His followers were filled with the Holy Spirit and empowered to proclaim deliverance and release captives wherever they went. In effect, they were empowered to declare the year of Jubilee and the new Law of God. The law of Freedom; the law of a people justified by faith. For that reason, church can and should be a continuous Jubilee celebration.

So, how does this relate to revival? Revival is Pentecost! It is an extraordinary, wild mix of God's righteous law being revealed, but also God's Spirit being poured out on all flesh. It is the completeness of grace. In revival, we have it all! People are convicted of their sin. Those who didn't know God's righteous standard suddenly see they are sinners, guilty before a holy God and eternally condemned. Sometimes in revival when Charles Finney was preaching people would actually start to experience hell and come running in repentance to the altar begging God for forgiveness. That would be a Mount Sinai experience! But then as they come in repentance, God washed away their sin with the blood of Jesus and filled them with His glorious Holy Spirit, releasing them from slavery, forgiving all their debts, and accepting them as sons, making them co-heirs with Christ to His eternal riches... that would be the upper room Jerusalem experience! Eternal riches instead of eternal condemnation; is that not complete grace!

Take Mount Sinai, the upper room experience, and the year of Jubilee and put them in a blender—what do you have? You have revival. Revival, like the law and the Holy Spirit, is complete grace. It is God coming down and revealing His righteous standard, but then not leaving us powerless before it. Instead, he redeems us with His blood, filling us gloriously with His Spirit so that we can proclaim Jubilee to everyone, heal the sick and set captives free. When we pray for revival, we are asking for the fullness of Pentecost—both Old and New Testament Pentecost—to be released upon our city. We are praying for the Jubilee year to become our reality.

And so we pray...

Lord, I bow my heart and bend my knee,
send revival, and start with me;
Pour out your Spirit in an unprecedented way;
May all who hear be saved today;
May all who are saved proclaim the Way;
Lord send revival and start with me.

Add some ink: *My thoughts and prayers on this day;*

_____

_____

_____

_____

_____

DAY 36

Treasure Hunting

*Again, the kingdom of heaven is like treasure hidden in a field,
which a man found and hid; and for joy over it, he goes and sells all
that he has and buys that field. Again, the kingdom of heaven is like
a merchant seeking beautiful pearls, who, when he had found one
pearl of great price, went and sold all that he had and bought it.*
MATTHEW 13:44-46 NKJV

We have heard that when revival comes, people travel from all over the world to be a part of it. They buy airplane tickets, book hotels, leave jobs and even move cities—just to be part of it. Why? Because there is nothing better this side of heaven than living in revival! There is no price you can put on revival. It is God himself coming near. Is this not the most important, exciting, and valuable thing that could ever happen? It is most certainly worth seeking!

In the Gospel of Matthew Chapter 13:44-46, Jesus tells us the value of His kingdom, His presence, His rule, and reign here on earth. He explains that it is worth more than anything else we could own. When the people in Jesus' parable found the treasure in the field and the pearl of great price, they sold everything to have it.

It reminds me of the story of Obed-Edom in second Samuel. When the Ark of the Covenant was placed in his care, we are told that in just three months his house was so radically blessed that everyone could see the difference! We are not sure exactly what the

     W. Samuel Sandeman

blessing looked like, but I like to think that revival came to his house.

When King David saw the blessing on Obed-Edom, he took the ark from Obed-Edom and brought it to Jerusalem. But Obed-Edom had tasted something. In those three months, he found something worth giving his whole life for. He packed up his house and moved to Jerusalem just to stay close to the ark. He took up the role of being a doorkeeper and gatekeeper in the tabernacle just so he could be around it. He then became a musician and worship leader because being a doorkeeper wasn't close enough. God gave him eight sons and all his sons and grandsons also committed to taking up roles around the ark.

Obed-Edom found the pearl of great price. It was the presence of God on earth. He paid whatever price he could for it and built his entire life around stewarding it. Such is the kingdom of God!

Can we put a price on a soul being saved? Can we put a price on a heart being healed? A life being changed? Blind eyes (both spiritual and physical) opening? Cripples walking? Cancers disappearing? A man or woman set free from addiction, depression, or demonic oppression? What about the fullness of peace and joy we experience in His presence? These are the treasures of the kingdom and they are worth seeking!

Have you noticed that these treasures of the kingdom do not just lie around everywhere? In the same way that gold and oil do not just lie around, these treasures have to be sought after and sought out.

Our Lord Jesus said the kingdom of God is *"like a merchant seeking beautiful pearls."* Merchants back then were people who travelled to distant lands looking for things of value. They were professional treasure hunters. Paying whatever price to find treasure. In our pursuit of revival, we must be like these merchants of old.

Our prayer posture should reflect the example of their lives. We must dig in the spirit until we find the wells of old. We must press on, even though we feel we have found nothing to date. We must persistently press in because revival does not just lie around, it must be sought intentionally with endurance.

Modern-day treasure hunters would be those commissioning massive rigs to drill the depths of the oceans to find oil, or miners coring kilometres deep into the earth to find gold, platinum, and diamonds. Huge cost, huge effort, tremendous risk, but they do it because they know the value of what they are looking for.

Saints we need to remind ourselves of the value of what we are searching for! As we pray for revival we are like merchants of old, we are like modern-day treasure hunters, but the treasure we seek is of infinitely more valuable than theirs.

So, let's continue to seek the treasures of the kingdom of God!

And so we pray...

Lord, I bow my heart and bend my knee,
send revival, and start with me;
Pour out your Spirit in an unprecedented way;
May all who hear be saved today;
May all who are saved proclaim the Way;
Lord send revival and start with me.

Add some ink: *My thoughts and prayers on this day;*

_____

_____

_____

_____

_____

DAY 37

Spiritual Tenders

I keep asking that the God of our Lord Jesus Christ, the Father of glory, may give to you the spirit of wisdom and revelation in the knowledge of Him, that the eyes of your understanding being enlightened; that you may know what is the hope of His calling, what are the riches of the glory of His inheritance in the saints, and what is the exceeding greatness of His power toward us who believe, according to the working of His mighty power.
EPHESIANS 1:17-19 NKJV

Paul prayed a powerful prayer for the believers in Ephesus which is recorded for our benefit:

He prayed for them to have revelation knowledge of three things:

1. The power-filled life they were called to live as Christians
2. How rich with glory they were
3. The greatness of God's power toward them

I do not want to get to the end of my life on earth or even step into eternity and only then find out what I could have had or experienced with God. Do you? I want revelation and understanding of what is ours in Christ, whilst on planet earth. Paul was praying this for the Ephesian church: *"Lord, give them revelation knowledge of what an power-filled life they are called to live, how rich they are with glory and how great your power is toward them..."* Paul understood that if they

W. Samuel Sandeman

don't have revelation knowledge of these things they will not enter into or experience them.

During the Second World War, General Wainwright of the US army was held captive as a prisoner of war in Japan, even after the Japanese had surrendered to the US. How is that possible? Quite simply because he didn't know. He didn't know the war had been won and his captors certainly weren't going to tell him! He didn't know that his freedom had been purchased. However, when news came that he was indeed free and the war had been won, he rose in authority and took charge of that P.O.W. camp and claimed his freedom.

The moment that somebody realises with revelation knowledge the power-filled life that God has called us to live, how rich we are with glory, and the greatness of God's power that is available to us—that is the moment things can change. Without that revelation or understanding, we carry on unemployed, broke, sick or captive.

When a government releases a tender for work that needs to be carried out in the city, it is required to publish the tender for all to see. The responsibility then rests on companies to apply. There are conditions to be met in the applications, but somebody must put their hand up and say, *'I want the work!'* and then apply for it. In order to make that decision, somebody needs to see that the tender has been published. They need to know about it and understand the scope, requirements and potential benefits of the tender.

The same is true with revival: God has published in His Word that He will pour out His Spirit on all flesh—His sons and His daughters WILL prophesy (Joel 2). He has promised times of refreshing (Acts 3). He has published that His name will be great in the nations (Malachi 1). He has promised to clothe His disciples with power from on high (Acts 1). But what we learn from history is that somebody has to put up their hand and apply for these spiritual tenders.

How we need a revelation that there is a tender for revival! It is available, God can and will move as He did at Pentecost, in Herrnhut, Wales, the Hebrides, Zululand, Brownsville, Toronto, Azusa, PyongYang and so many other places… in fact, I'm sure there is a tender for revival with your city's name on it!

So many of us do not have revelation knowledge that there are such wonderful, profitable spiritual tenders available. We only sometimes hear of the move of God. Most of the time we think the people to whom it happened were just lucky or it was just some random stroke of divine grace that saw God move so powerfully in their generation. What we don't hear is that in every case somebody heard what was available, believed it was for them, and then applied for it. Without doing that we are like a company with no order book, waiting for work, not knowing there is a tender with our name on it.

I hope that over the last five weeks of prayer and devotion you have grown in revelation knowledge of revival. I pray you are beginning to see that God indeed wants to pour out His Spirit on us, because He is a good Father, for whom it is a pleasure to give the Kingdom to His children. That has been our prayer for you as you have worked through this book and prayed for revival. Remember that Hebrews Chapter 11 teaches that God rewards those that diligently seek Him. You have diligently sought after Him, now expect a reward from Him, even His Holy Spirit and His glory.

Once we have revelation knowledge that it is there for us the question is then how do we apply? With tenders there are always conditions. We have looked at many conditions for "spiritual tenders" including faith in God's goodness, hunger for His Word and thirst for His Spirit. We spoke about extra-ordinary prayer, heartfelt, insistent, audacious prayer. We spoke about the necessary

W. Samuel Sandeman

ingredients of repentance, humility, obedience, consistency, and even drawing near in holiness.

One expression of faith we have not mentioned is that of fasting. Fasting is a powerful expression of our hunger and thirst for revival. Fasting is powerful because it has the ingredients of repentance, humility, and obedience. We have three more days before our 40 days are complete. I want to invite you to finish this devotional with a three-day fast for revival in your city and your church. Ending with a fast will be significant! (See Annexure 1 at the end of this book for some suggested guidelines on fasting.)

Let us pray that God will continue to give us revelation knowledge of what is available to us, and as He anoints your holy imagination with visions of what is possible when He comes near to your city, begin to pray those visions out with the same authority that General Wainwright took on himself when he realised that he was on the side that won. For the battle belongs to YHWH, and in Christ Jesus, we are more than conquerors!

And so we pray...

Lord, I bow my heart and bend my knee,
send revival, and start with me;
Pour out your Spirit in an unprecedented way;
May all who hear be saved today;
May all who are saved proclaim the Way;
Lord send revival and start with me.

Add some ink: *My thoughts and prayers on this day;*

_____

_____

_____

_____

DAY 38

Our Great Need

Then he turned toward the woman and said to Simon, "Do you see this woman? I came into your house. You did not give me any water for my feet, but she wet my feet with her tears and wiped them with her hair. You did not give me a kiss, but this woman, from the time I entered, has not stopped kissing my feet. You did not put oil on my head, but she has poured perfume on my feet. Therefore, I tell you, her many sins have been forgiven—as her great love has shown. But those who assume they have very little to be forgiven will love me very little.
LUKE 7:44-47 NIV

This story is a beautiful picture of love, or "great love" as Jesus called it. This woman knew what she needed. She needed forgiveness. She was a prostitute. How and why she became a prostitute we don't know, but her notoriety as such was clearly established.

She went into Simon's house and crashed his well-to-do dinner party to perform this act of great love. Simon was a well-known Pharisee, so she certainly wasn't invited and everyone, as well as her, knew that, but she didn't care—she was going to get to Jesus no matter what.

It was obviously pre-meditated. She came prepared with the perfume, she knew what she was going to do and she did it.

Something must have happened in her life, some sort of spiritual awakening. Maybe she was in Jesus' meetings, maybe she heard Him preach or saw His miracles. We don't know, but her heart was broken for her sins and she knew she had to change.

She knew she would be scorned by the guests there. She knew their eyes would all be glaring at her. She knew she might even be thrown out, but she did it anyway. She humbled herself at Jesus' feet, wept, and poured out her perfume on Him.

The room at that moment was filled with two contrasting aromas, that of arrogant shock and that of her sweet repentant perfume. I imagine the typical sound of dinner plates clanging and the table chatter that normally fills the air at dinner parties coming to an abrupt end when she entered. There must have been a very uneasy silence in the room as she went to her knees before Jesus. However, the shock of all shocks was before someone could throw her out, Jesus received her, honoured her, and made an example of her, praising her actions.

Just as much as they did not expect a prostitute to crash the dinner party, no one expected Jesus to react the way He did. He was not embarrassed by a prostitute perfuming and cleaning his feet with her tears. Your average rabbi would not even walk on the same side of the road as her. Your typical religious leader would recoil in disgust at her presence. But not Jesus. He tenderly received her.

Why? Why would he do that? Because He knew her. Not just about her, her reputation. He knew *her* and she was the reason why He came. He came to save, to heal, to forgive, and to redeem lives.

The shock for the guests wasn't over, the dinner party wasn't completely ruined at that moment, but when Jesus turned to Simon, the man who owned the house and organised the party, the host of the evening, the respectable and admired Pharisee and leader, and began to chastise him for not doing the same, *"you did*

not give me water for my feet, a kiss, or oil for my head, but she did..."
I'm sure at that moment most of the guests would have wanted to just disappear.

The big difference between the woman and Simon is that she knew her condition and he did not know his. He was also in need of forgiveness and a personal revival. He was no different from the woman, but religion had anaesthetised him into thinking he was ok. By thinking he was ok, he was not able to access the anointing for transformation that Jesus carried.

Could this be a picture of some churches today? We have Jesus at our 'parties' but we are not accessing the power of His Spirit because we do not see our deep need? Maybe we too have been anaesthetised by our cultural Christianity and abundance of religious stuff, leaving us with a veneer of Christianity, but in reality, we are no different to the world. Like Simon we have Jesus in our house, but we are uninvolved in God's mission to save and redeem the world, more concerned with our nice parties than the brokenness right outside our front doors.

Saints if we are not supernaturally awakened to know how much we need Jesus or the power of His Spirit we go without it. Like Simon, we have Him at our church services, but we don't access the anointing that releases salvation, forgiveness, healing, deliverance, or redemption. This dinner party drama serves as a powerful lesson if we are indeed anything like Simon. We must change our posture and become like the woman.

Revival came to the woman because by the grace of God she was supernaturally awakened to her great need and she knew Jesus was the answer. We do not know what happened to Simon, maybe after that encounter and rebuke, he too was supernaturally awakened to his great need. We hope revival came to him, but we know it came to her.

So, let us do what the woman did, let this fast and our commitment to prayer that we are engaged in be a picture of her posture, let it be an act of humility, desperation, determination, and "great love" because we see OUR great need for Jesus to come and fill us with His Spirit and make us as we should be.

And so we pray...

> Lord, I bow my heart and bend my knee,
> send revival, and start with me;
> Pour out your Spirit in an unprecedented way;
> May all who hear be saved today;
> May all who are saved proclaim the Way;
> Lord send revival and start with me.

Add some ink: *My thoughts and prayers on this day;*

_____

_____

_____

_____

_____

DAY 39

New Wine

Where there is new wine, There is new power
There is new freedom...
NEW WINE BY HILLSONG MUSIC

...Nor do they put new wine into old wineskins, or else the wineskins break, the wine is spilled, and the wineskins are ruined. But they put new wine into new wineskins, and both are preserved.
MATTHEW 9:17 NKJV

This Jesus said in response to a question about why His ministry did not look like the ministry of the Pharisees or John the Baptist. They were fasting, but Jesus and His motley crew were not fasting. In fact, Jesus was accused of being a glutton by some.

The new wine Jesus was talking about was the New Covenant and the ministry of the Holy Spirit that He was instituting. Jesus brought a whole lot of "new" into view! Through Him, God abandoned the Temple built with hands and made people His dwelling place. He burst out of the centripetal pattern of operation we know as the Old Testament and flooded the nations with His acceptance and benevolence. Did you notice one of the last things that Jesus says in the book of Revelation is "Behold, I make all things new!"?

Jesus introduced the word 'church' instead of 'synagogue.' He gave us a five-fold, gift-based ministry instead of scribes and priests. And then to really shake things up He made all believers priests. He made a complete overhaul of methods, modes, structures, systems, and leadership. He made a new wineskin, to contain new wine.

Wine is symbolic of the life and power of the Holy Spirit, who is synonymous with the presence and favour of God. Wineskins are the structures that contain the wine. The wineskins symbolise all the systems and ways we organise and relate to each other. The church is the wineskin, and the Holy Spirit is the wine. It is possible to have a wineskin with no wine; a church with systems and organisation, but no power, might, or presence. The Bible describes it as "having a form of godliness but denying the power therein" (2 Timothy 3:5).

We too, as individuals, are wineskins. We are the containers of God's anointing and power, and it is possible we too can have all the structure of Christian life, yet no presence and power of the Holy Spirit living within us and through us. When we as individuals or churches have systems, but no power what we need is revival. Revival is the arrival of new wine.

There is a pattern we see in history where we go from 'wine' to 'no wine' to 'new wine'. We see this at the wedding in Cana—they had wine, then they had no wine, and then came the new wine (John 2:1-12). Wine does run out, and for so many reasons; there are anointings for different times and seasons, but sometimes it is just not stewarded diligently. Whatever the reason, when the wine runs out and is gone, it is an important time. When the wine has gone, we must know it has gone and we must start looking for new wine. If we don't, we just stay as an old wineskin holding on to old things that carry no life or godly power.

At the same time, we must make sure that we become a new wineskin that can contain the new wine we are seeking. Old

W. Samuel Sandeman

wineskins are not thrown away, they can and must be renewed and repurposed. How are old wineskins renewed? You take the skin and submerge it in water for some time. Then you massage oil into it making it soft and flexible again.

We can as individuals and churches be renewed by submerging ourselves in seasons of prayer and the word, and then going through deep repentance making our hearts soft and flexible to the Holy Spirit so that He is integrated and very much a part of every aspect of our lives again. This is the purpose of this 40-day devotional and especially this time fasting. As you have journeyed through the last 38 days, you have been immersed in the process of becoming a new wineskin. As you are fasting, you are emptying yourself to be filled by the Holy Spirit; to have the oil of joy and gladness massaged into every aspect of your life, that you may faithfully hold the new wine that God will pour out.

So, as you pray this morning, ask the Lord to continue to renew and repurpose you and your community so that you can be ready for new wine. Have a heart that says, *"Lord if there is anything that needs to change so the Holy Spirit and I can be in deep fellowship again, then change it. Change my speech, my time with you, the way I live day in and day out. I put it all on the altar, on your altar. I offer myself as a living sacrifice. Make me new and fill me with new wine."*

In the words of the song 'New Wine' by Hillsong music:

Make me Your vessel
Make me an offering
Make me whatever You want me to be
I came here with nothing
But all You have given me
Jesus bring new wine out of me

If we can posture our hearts in such surrender, there is the promise of new wine,

> *Where there is new wine*
> *There is new power*
> *There is new freedom*
> *The Kingdom is here*

How true! When there is new wine there is new power and new freedom—there is revival. Do you need some 'new'? Jesus, offers you a new touch, a fresh start, a new freedom, a new power to do life. He can touch you right now, He can fill you and your church with new wine. He can make all things new for you, receive it by faith!

And so we pray...

> *Lord, I bow my heart and bend my knee,*
> *send revival, and start with me;*
> *Pour out your Spirit in an unprecedented way;*
> *May all who hear be saved today;*
> *May all who are saved proclaim the Way;*
> *Lord send revival and start with me.*

Add some ink: *My thoughts and prayers on this day;*

_____

_____

_____

_____

DAY 40

Do it Again

You made a way, where there was no way
And I believe, I'll see You do it again
DO IT AGAIN BY ELEVATION WORSHIP

Here we are on Day 40 of praying for revival. We are also on Day 3 of fasting for revival! I hope this has been a significant journey for you and your community. I also hope that you are hungry; hungry for God. As we wrap this devotional journey, I want to encourage you keep on in your prayer for revival. I hope you have discovered a treasure worth pursuing and that you will continue to rise early (or stay up late) and pray <u>until</u> you and your community experience the promise.

There is a scripture verse that I have been saving for this final day of devotions, it is a prayer found in the 3rd chapter of Habakkuk. When this prayer was made the Jews in Judah were on the edge of disaster. Evil was prospering, spirituality was at an all-time low, the northern kingdom had already been destroyed and the Babylonian invasion was imminent. What do God's people do in such times? They turn to prayer as Habakkuk did in Chapter 3, verse 2. The NIV translation writes it as this:

Lord, I have heard of your fame;
I stand in awe of your deeds, Lord.
Repeat them in our day,
in our time make them known;
in wrath remember mercy.

The New Living Translation (NLT) translates it as:

I have heard all about you, Lord.
I am filled with awe by your amazing works.
In this time of our deep need, help us again
as you did in years gone by...

I want to look more intently at that wonderful prayer because it is a prayer for revival. As we look around at our world does it not seem like we too are on the edge of disaster? Evil is prospering no doubt about that. In such times the appropriate action is to turn to God and seek Him like Habakkuk did.

The prophet says; "*I have heard all about you and I am filled with awe by your amazing works...*"

In a time of great need, Habakkuk immersed himself in God's testimonies: "*I have heard all about you and your works.*" I'm sure there were other things to hear that he could have given his ear to. There must have been plenty news of the impending invasion or the disaster and tragedy of the northern kingdom. But he said, "*I have heard all about You!*" I imagine while the world was in an uproar all around him, Habakkuk was studying revivals, learning how God moved in previous generations, giving attention to what God had done—in essence reading God's newspaper rather than the world's. And it sounds to me like all his hearing resulted in a heart that was expectant for a move of God: *"I am filled with awe by your amazing works."*

Knowing how God has moved in previous generations is so important. In numerous instances in the Bible, God exhorts His people to tell one another of His wonderful works and the glorious things that He has done. When we know these stories and testimonies, we can be filled with faith and hope for Him to do the same in our generation. If we don't hear these stories, repeat them to others, study them, or let them fill our imagination, then we, unfortunately, default to the status quo and we don't carry the necessary faith to see change. In this revival devotion, you have heard of how God has moved in various places around the world, but we have only touched the smallest tip of the iceberg—there are so many more stories and testimonies and I encourage you to go dig for more. YouTube is a wonderful resource, where you can find footage of the revivals in Toronto, Pensacola (Brownsville), Indonesia and Alma Longa; the transformations of cities as found in the "Transformations" videos from the 1990s. You can also find interviews of people who were alive during the Azusa Street revival and experienced the sweetness of God's glorious presence there, as well as stories and documentaries on the Welsh revivals, the Moravian revival, the miracle of '94 in South Africa, the miracle of Dunkirk, etc etc. There are other websites that we have referred to in this devotional, as well as many other online resources and books. Find them, study them, meditate on them, pray into them.

God has moved before, He has done amazing works in pockets all over the world, and this is our surety that things can be different for us. God can help us again. God can invade your city and put your church supernaturally on the front foot again. He can fill your community with power and enable you to be witnesses and ambassadors. The lame can walk again, the blind can see, a half-hearted compromised church can be revived into a powerful force in society, the hardened can come to repentance, sinners can pursue holiness, Christians can walk with boldness, we can experience joy, the lost can be found, a whole city can be changed, the ends of the earth can be reached, God's presence can come near, we can taste heaven on earth; *"I AM FILLED WITH AWE BY YOUR AMAZING WORKS!"*

Habakkuk allowed these testimonies to fill him with awe! In a time when the world was on the edge of disaster, he was consumed with what God could do, and asked God to "do it again!". We too must be a people filled with holy awe of what God has done and what He can do.

What do we do with our awe? We translate it into intercession as the prophet did; *"In this time of our deep need, help us again as you did in years gone by..."* He carried a prayer and hunger that said *"Lord, do it again!"*

There is a song by Elevation Church that goes like this:

Your promise still stands
Great is Your faithfulness, I'm still in Your hands
This is my confidence, You never failed me yet
I've seen You move, come move the mountains
And I believe, I'll see You do it again
You made a way, where there was no way
And I believe, I'll see You do it again

This was Habakkuk's prayer; "Lord do it again!" This is the prayer we must continue to carry and steward; *"Lord do it again, do it now, do it in my church, do it in my city."*

Jesus instructed us in Matthew 6:33 to seek first the kingdom of God. I like the way it says it in the Passion Translation:

So above all, constantly chase after the realm of God's
kingdom and the righteousness that proceeds from him.
MATTHEW 6:33 TPT

I love that; *"constantly chase after the realm of God's kingdom!"* This is the instruction I want to leave with you: ...*above all, constantly chase after the realm of God's kingdom.*

Saints we need a move of God, let us be the people who are filled with awe of what God can do, and who constantly chase after the realm of His kingdom crying, "Lord do it again!"

And so we pray...

Lord, I bow my heart and bend my knee,
send revival, and start with me;
Pour out your Spirit in an unprecedented way;
May all who hear be saved today;
May all who are saved proclaim the Way;
Lord send revival and start with me.

Add some ink: *My thoughts and prayers on this day;*

_____

_____

_____

_____

_____

W. Samuel Sandeman

Suggestions for the Three-Day Fast

If you have not fasted before, then it is good to "ease into it" rather than shock your body.

We suggest the following:

1. **Preparation**: Try to reduce processed foods, coffee and eliminate red meat the day before you fast. Increase your intake of roughage, vegetables and fruit, and drink plenty of water. This will help you to "detox" and prepare your body for what is to come.
2. **Day 1:** Cut out all meats, bread and processed foods. Eat only vegetables and fruit. If you need to, eat some rice, sweet potato or other root vegetables. Most importantly, set aside time to pray. Kennedy Bongani used to say, "Fasting without prayer is just starvation." Read a chapter of your Bible in the morning, at noon and night. And pray each time you read it. Oh, and did we mention, spend time praying. Pray for yourself, your family, your church leaders, your whole church, for your unsaved friends and colleagues and your city. Pray.
3. **Day 2**: Do the above, plus cut out all starch. Try to cut out your vegetables, only eating alkaline fruit, such as apples and pears. Cut out all citrus fruit. If you drink fruit juice, ensure that it diluted with water. Have your Bible close to you and read it whenever you get hungry, reminding yourself and the demonic realm that you do not "live by bread alone, but by every word that comes out of the mouth of God." Set

aside your normal mealtimes and teatimes to pray and read Scripture.

At night, turn off the TV, your cell phone and all social media and commit yourself to prayer. Your energy levels are usually lowest on Day 2. Push through. You may even feel queasy at times. Pray with groans, but pray always (Romans 8).

4. **Day 3**: As above, plus cut out <u>all</u> solids. If you get really hungry, sip some diluted fruit juice or herbal tea. You should start feeling stronger and more energetic on Day 3. If you are feeling good, why not push on to Day 4 and Day 5. Seek the Lord and subdue your flesh. And look out for breakthrough and answers to your prayers. God is faithful.

Through the fast, keep a journal of what Scriptures have been jumping out at you. Record dreams, visions, and anything else that you believe God has been saying. Also, be diligent to write down how God has answered your prayers as time goes on. It is easy to be like the Israelites in the Wilderness and forget the move of the hand of God over time. Write down the wonderful things that He has done and tell others of His goodness.

Prophetic Words to Church Leaders in 2022

In the lead up to the publishing of this book, God was seen to be in the process of raising up small bands of prayer warriors around the city where we live, and beyond.

Through the prayer times, the Holy Spirit spoke a number of words of exhortation that encouraged the groups to keep praying for revival. There were a few words that were directed to church leaders with regards to the coming revival. Here are some that seem to be key words from God:

1. **New Wine Skins / New Piping:** As in the early 1990s, prior to the move of the Spirit that resulted in the Toronto Blessing, the Pensacola Revival and the revival in Holy Trinity Brompton, there was a word that has been reiterated at this time: "No-one pours new wine into old wine skins." God wants His church leaders to put a new skin on their church to prepare the way to contain the results of the move of the Spirit. Here in some parts of Durban, we see a parallel analogy: burst water pipes. In certain of the older neighbourhoods of the city, burst water pipes have been a daily occurrence, resulting in roads collapsing and supply of water to households being cut off, whilst rivers of water run down the streets. God is saying: *"My living waters are plentiful, but your structures are old and broken and cannot contain the pressure of the flow of my Holy Spirit. Renew your structures; lay new pipelines, so that my living waters can flow to my people that they may drink and be cleansed by my Spirit. If you rely on your old structures, they will break, and the people*

will be thirsty. They will be forced to drink stagnant water and "bottled" water, but miss the fresh, living waters of my Holy Spirit."

2. **The Ceiling of Worship:** There have been several words from different sources indicating that worship will be a key factor in this revival. God is wanting to manifest His glory amongst His people. He wants His glory to be <u>upon</u> His people. He has said that this will happen through worship. He has prophesied that the glass ceilings that have been over the worship leaders in this season will be broken; that worship leaders will no longer be constrained in their worship. It is God's will that we worship Him in Spirit and in truth, that we enter His presence and revel in His presence. New songs will come out of this; new songs to bless the nations.

3. **Pass the Mantle, Empower the Next Generation:** Possibly as part of the "new wine skins" or "new structures" church leaders are being called to empower the next generation, not just through teaching and training them, but by blessing them and authorising them to move and minister under the authority of Christ. There are many church leaders with gifting and anointing from the Holy Spirit that they need to "give away" to the next generation. You need to be like Elijah and pass the mantle to your Elisha. There are ministries that you need to give away so that God can give you more. In a similar word, we have felt that God is wanting to do a work through the youth, particularly those in the age group of 14 to 17, but also stretching into young adults. He intends to raise up a young army to take this next generation.

4. **Preach the Gospel:** A revival is normally a movement of the Spirit that results in a great harvest of souls. We feel that God is saying, in preparation for revival, "*Do the work of an evangelist. Preach the Gospel in season and out of season. This is not the time for the harvest, but the season for the harvest is coming, and those that have shown themselves as faithful to preach the Gospel and do the work of an evangelist in this season will reap a bountiful harvest in the season that is to come.*"

Made in United States
Orlando, FL
27 April 2024

46234329R00114